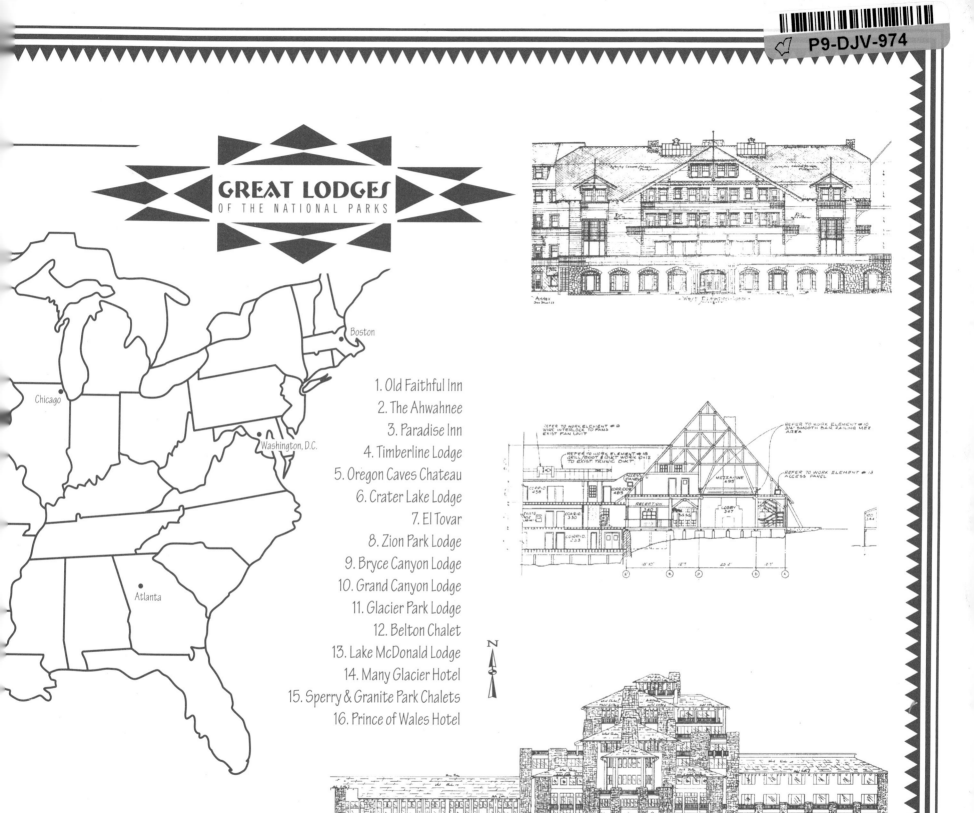

GREAT LODGES
OF THE NATIONAL PARKS

Boston

Chicago

Washington, D.C.

Atlanta

1. Old Faithful Inn
2. The Ahwahnee
3. Paradise Inn
4. Timberline Lodge
5. Oregon Caves Chateau
6. Crater Lake Lodge
7. El Tovar
8. Zion Park Lodge
9. Bryce Canyon Lodge
10. Grand Canyon Lodge
11. Glacier Park Lodge
12. Belton Chalet
13. Lake McDonald Lodge
14. Many Glacier Hotel
15. Sperry & Granite Park Chalets
16. Prince of Wales Hotel

N

2/14/15

"(Happy Valentines Day, Boyd!"

With great fondness and enduring gratitude for your warm friendship and unconditional & loving support. You have been my Valentine and I shall be forever in your debt. In your manner and devotion to social grace your are a living symbol of "hospitality" and "generosity." God bless you, dear Boyd.

In Christian love,

George Taylor

GREAT LODGES
OF THE NATIONAL PARKS

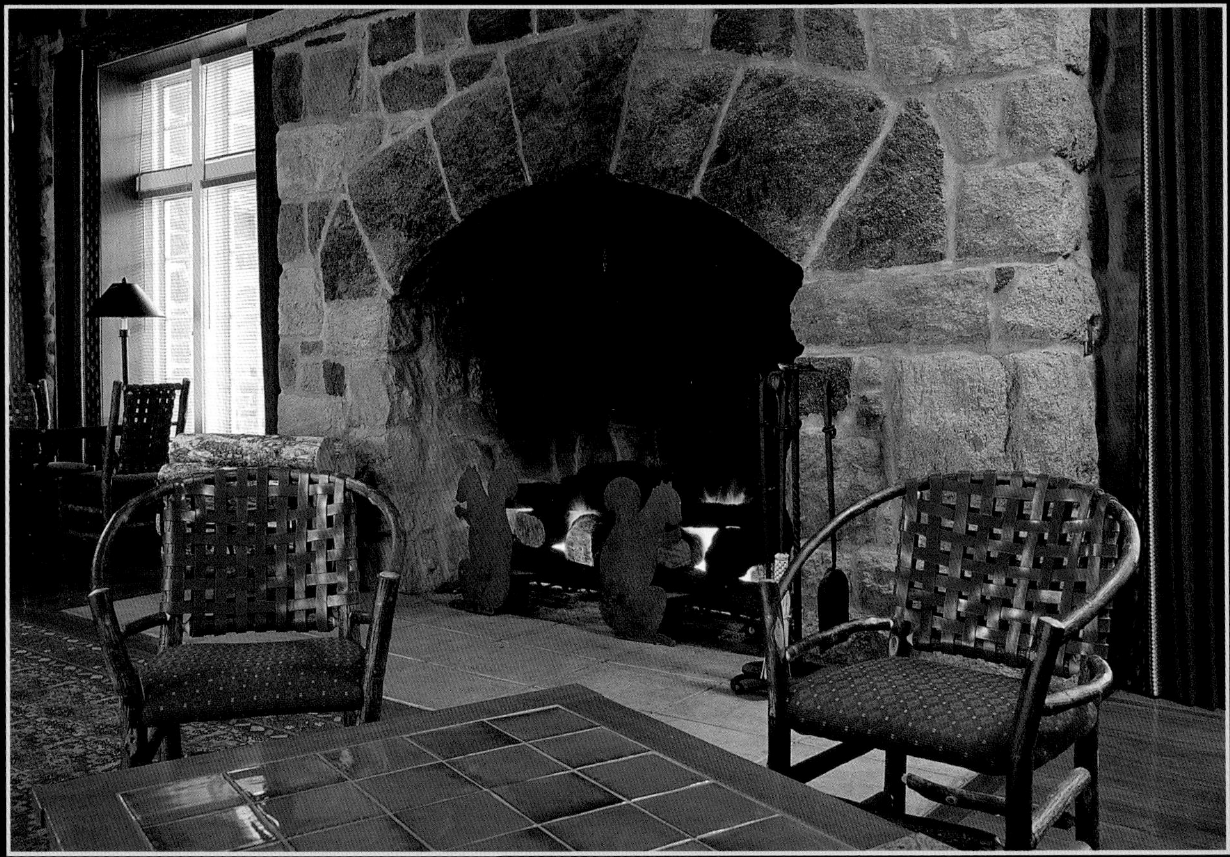

BY   CHRISTINE   BARNES
PHOTOGRAPHY BY FRED PFLUGHOFT & DAVID MORRIS

THE COMPANION BOOK TO THE   PBS TELEVISION SERIES

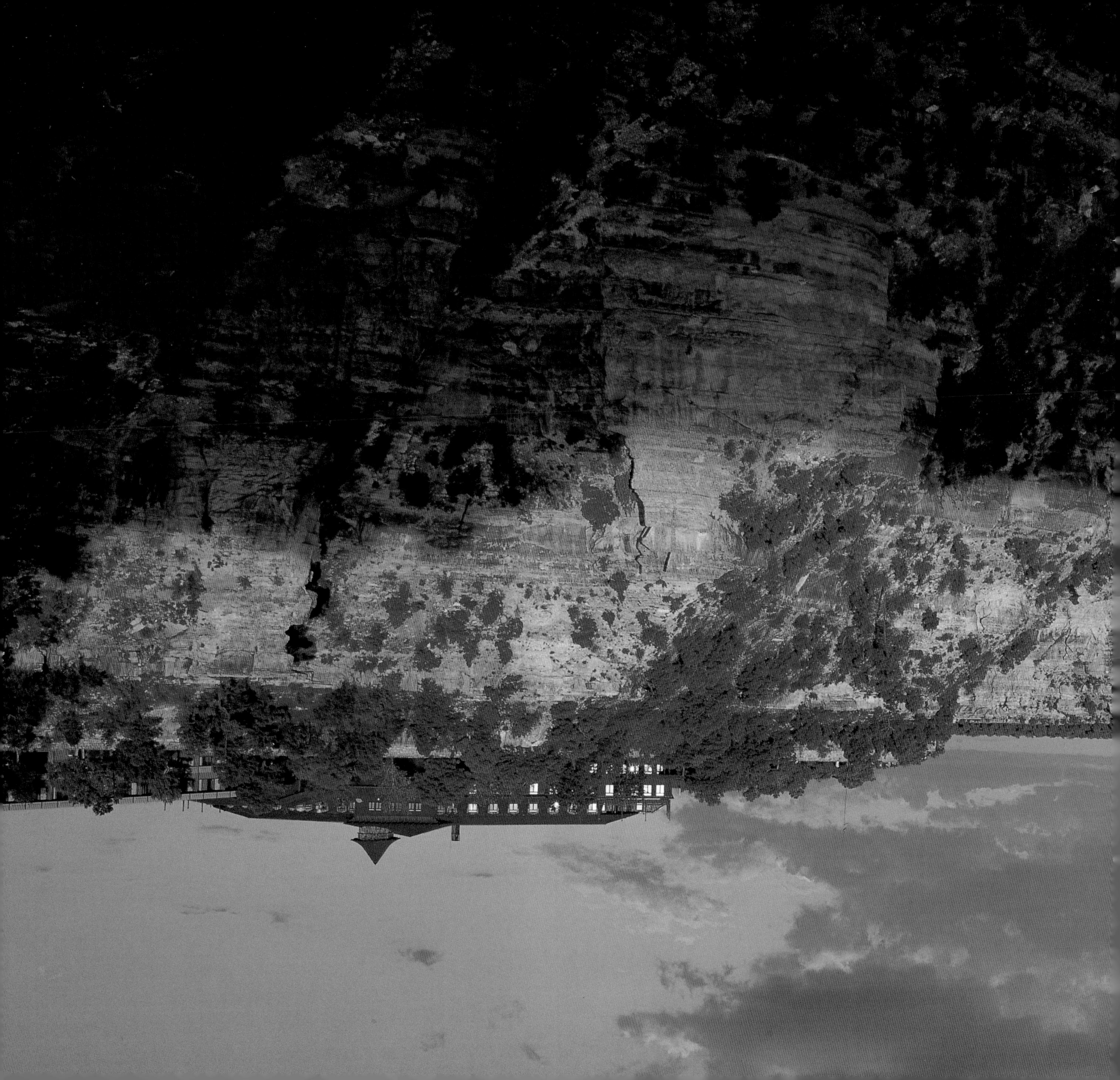

A SPECIAL THANK YOU
TO OUR GENEROUS FUNDERS
OF THE PBS TELEVISION SERIES,
THE ARTHUR VINING DAVIS FOUNDATIONS
AND M.J. MURDOCK CHARITABLE TRUST.

First Edition, Eighth Printing
Published by W.W.West, Inc., 20875 Sholes Rd., Bend, Oregon

Text copyright 2002 by Christine Barnes
Photos copyright 2002 by photographers credited

Book Design: Linda McCray
Copy Editor: Barbara Fifer

Publisher's Cataloging-in-Publication Data
Barnes, Christine 1947-
    Great Lodges of the National Parks/Christine Barnes
    photographs by Fred Pflughoft and David Morris--
    1st edition
    p.cm.
    includes bibliographical references
    ISBN: 0-9653924-5-7

1. National Parks and Reserves--West (U.S.)
2. Historical Buildings--West (U.S.)
3. Hotels--West (U.S.) Guidebooks I. Title

Library of Congress catalog card number
Printed in China by C & C Offset Printing Co. Ltd.

*The great hall was part of Crater lake Lodge's rehabilitation,
Crater Lake National Park, Oregon, title page.*

*El Tovar washed by the setting sun, Grand Canyon National
Park, Arizona, pages 2-3.*

*Mount Rainier looms behind Paradise Inn, Mount Rainier
National Park, Washington, right.*

FOR JERRY,
WHO ALWAYS INSPIRES ME
AND
MELISSA, SANJAY,
MICHAEL, KAREN, AND JACKSON

The acknowledgments for this project could fill another book, but first I want to thank my publisher, Don Compton, without whom none of my lodge books or this program would have been possible.

Fred Pflughoft and David Morris captured the lodges' and parks' beauty in their photographs, Barbara Fifer edited the text with a deft touch, and Linda McCray brought the words and images together with her incredible design skills.

My gratitude to the historians, archivists, and park personnel who pointed me in the right directions, answered endless questions and shared their knowledge. Among them are Linny Adamson, Richard Bartlett, Andy Beck, Jan Balsom, Tessie Bundick, Gordon Chappel, Linda Eade, Ann Emmons, Mark Herberger, Laurin Huffman III, Bob Jacobs, Jeff Jaqua, Steve Mark, Henry Matthews, James McDonald, Paul Newman, Deirdre Shaw, Jim Sndyer, and John Roth. Thanks goes to each individual who shared a story here and in the PBS program, and to the lodge managers and staffs who showed old-fashioned hospitality that Fred Harvey would have been proud of.

My thanks also go to executive producer John Grant of Driftwood Productions, and Oregon Public Broadcasting, including Maynard Orme and John Lindsay.

I especially want to thank John Booth, Mark Mitchell, Steve Heiser, and Carolyn Zelle, along with their associates Pauline Reimer, Lori Gomez, Thea Bergeron, and Donna Matrazzo, for the pleasure of working with them. And most of all for letting me revisit these special places through their eyes.

AUTHOR'S NOTE

Great Lodges of the National Parks was a unique opportunity for me. As consultant and historian for the PBS series of the same name, and author of this companion book, I had an opportunity to see old familiar places through new eyes and expand the story of this country's most important historic architecture set amidst our greatest natural wonders.

My interest in America's grand old lodges began as a weekend trip to the re-opening of Oregon's Crater Lake Lodge in 1995 and evolved into my first lodge book, *Great Lodges of the West.*

Great Lodges of the National Parks builds on that saga and presents the story of the establishment of our national parks and the early development that made them accessible to those willing to venture into the relatively unknown. As Teddy Roosevelt once claimed, the best idea America ever had was its national parks.

Within these parks are remarkable shelters, but what seems most remarkable is that they still offer refuge to guests who bring the tales of the day's explorations into the great halls and dining rooms where they relive the wonders just outside the door.

Many of the lodges were financed by rail barons and designed by eager young architects willing to take a chance and create rustic designs that fit snugly with their setting. By the time the National Park Service was established in 1916, the notion of buildings that blended with the environment seemed as natural as the landscapes. Working in nearly inaccessible locations, railroad crews, masons and carpenters, landscape designers, businessmen and local boosters pooled their talent, resources, and determination to create these shelters. Structures collapsed during winter

storms, roads turned into bogs as wagons loaded with supplies sank into the mud; wind blew buildings out of plumb; financing vanished; and the desolate locations made every ordinary phase of construction an obstacle. Yet, they never gave up.

A perfect place to contemplate the drama of Old Faithful Inn is from the third floor balcony, above. Snow-draped trees frame The Ahwahnee, Yosemite National Park, California, facing page.

Decades later, the people who oversee, operate, maintain, and simply revel in the wonder of these lodges have their own stories to tell. Under the skilled direction of producers, cameramen, sound technicians, and editors, the people who care passionately about these buildings and parks give voice to what the first

director of the National Park Service, Stephen Mather observed: "People must see the parks to value them."

This book is a tactile reminder of all of those stories. Filled with the history of the lodges, it also includes authors, architects, historians, park rangers, and former employees whose lives have all been impacted by the lodges and parks they call home. Their words, from childhood memories to architectural analysis, enlighten readers as to why these buildings are so revered, and also convey why thousands of people work tirelessly to preserve them.

"It gets into your blood stream," explained Glacier National Park Superintendent Suzanne Lewis. "They are magnificent. You know how special they are. Today we would not build lodges like that especially in those locations. That makes them even more important as historic experiences and structures."

Returning to the lodges gave me a renewed sense that, indeed, these are far more than buildings, but reminders of our heritage. It also reaffirmed to me that the experience of hiking from Glacier Point with The Ahwahnee in full view 3,000 feet below, touching the hand-carved newel post at Timberline Lodge, or listening to someone like 86-year-old Harry Christiansen as he recalls the flood that nearly destroyed Oregon Caves Chateau are each experiences to be shared.

Great Lodges of the National Parks is for those whose memories keep the lodges alive, for those who head out into America's "best idea" to visit each remarkable lodge, and for those who find joy in learning about the history within our parks.

The Rendezvous Room of El Tovar retains its 1904 ambiance.

NATIONAL TRUST
for HISTORIC PRESERVATION

RICHARD MOE
PRESIDENT

FOREWORD

America's national parks, including those that are known primarily for their natural wonders, are liberally dotted with important older buildings. In all, the National Park Service is entrusted with responsibility for stewardship of more than 20,000 historic structures. Ranging from the Gilded Age mansions at Cumberland Island National Seashore to the weathered barns at a turn-of-the-century Mormon settlement in the shadow of the Grand Tetons to the unique visitors' facilities designed by Mary Colter for the Fred Harvey Company on the rim of the Grand Canyon, these structures are important, irreplaceable chapters in our nation's story. Among the best-known and best-loved of these treasures in brick, stone and timber are the lodges pictured in this book.

If the national parks are America's crowning glory, the national park lodges are among the brightest jewels in that crown. They delight us for many reasons: Yosemite's Ahwahnee would be a spectacular hotel even if it weren't set in a landscape of fabulous beauty. The Lake Yellowstone Hotel and Old Faithful Inn illustrate a dramatic change in attitude about what constitutes "appropriate" park architecture. Perhaps most intriguing of all, these places immerse us in a paradox: They celebrate the wilderness while swaddling us in creature comforts.

Sadly, the architectural significance and historical pedigree of these lodges, not to mention the affection in which they are held by millions of visitors, cannot protect them from the ravages of time, weather, budgetary restrictions and simple wear and tear. At Glacier National Park, the famed Many Glacier Hotel and two back-country chalets were in such deteriorated condition that they were included in the National Trust's 1996 list of America's 11 Most Endangered Historic Places. While conditions have improved at Glacier, the same threats – especially deferred maintenance – continue to plague historic structures in national parks from coast to coast.

We – and by "we" I mean all of us: Congress, the National Park Service, private concessionaires and members of the public – must work together to ensure that the needs of these landmarks are fully integrated into park planning, and that adequate funding is provided for their restoration and maintenance. We owe it to ourselves and to future generations to ensure that these proud, beautiful, history-rich pieces of the past will have a bright future.

Richard Moe

Protecting the Irreplaceable

1785 MASSACHUSETTS AVENUE, NW · WASHINGTON, DC 20036
202.588.6105 · FAX: 202.588.6082 · WWW.NATIONALTRUST.ORG

THE GRAND LODGES

Two of the West's most spectacular lodges lie in the hearts of Yellowstone and Yosemite national parks. The stories of Old Faithful Inn and of The Ahwahnee are the tales of two eras and their relationships with America's wilderness. Each stands as an example of man's ability to be part of the landscape he set aside to preserve.

Old Faithful Geyser and its namesake inn are natural and architectural landmarks in Yellowstone, America's first national park, above. Robert Reamer's drawings illustrate the asymmetrical design, facing page.

OLD FAITHFUL INN

OPENED 1904

There is a sense of frenzy at Yellowstone National Park. Each year three million visitors–high on the anticipation of encountering bison, bear, elk, moose, coyote, and wolves–visit America's first national park. The wildlife roam 2.2 million acres of mountainous, deeply gorged, fire-scarred, geyser-studded landscape interspersed with gentle meadows and meandering rivers.

Most visitors head to the Upper Geyser Basin to view the park's most famous geyser. By the time Old Faithful erupts, their adrenaline is pumped as high as the plumes of steam and scalding water that spew "like clockwork" 180 feet into the air. Then the crowd turns to Old Faithful Inn.

Moments after the geyser has erupted, the "geyser rush" takes over, and Old Faithful Inn is flooded with people. Visitors stream through the inn's massive red doors and walk under a low ceiling. Suddenly, the lobby opens up before them. "They're awestruck," said Leslie Quinn, who has shared that sense of awe since first coming to the park over twenty years ago. "Those who come here and step into the lobby of Old Faithful Inn find one of Yellowstone's greatest surprises."

Above them soars a tangle of trees forming an atrium that towers more than seventy-six feet. Square and diamond-shaped windowpanes filter light that plays amid the lodgepole pine poles and beams in the same way light changes in a forest. Balconies and stairways wind through the log columns and the gnarled knee-branch supports.

People stand there with their jaws hanging open.

And that would have made its architect Robert Chambers Reamer smile. Compared to traditional railway hotels of the era, Old Faithful Inn is radically different. While the inn features all of the amenities expected by a wealthy clientele of that time, it is not painted clapboard with fancy Victorian fretwork and fussy finials. With its western frontier sense of size, space, and grandeur, it is wildly rustic.

Even in 1902, when Reamer began designing the inn, the relatively unknown architect understood the draw of nature. He let the landscape introduce his creation, and he used the area's rough-and-tumble ingredients from which to build it. Hand-hewn, locally harvested logs cover the lower exterior, while wood shingles swathe the upper floors and steeply pitched roof. The inn's concrete foundation has a stone veneer quarried from the nearby Black Sand Basin. Chunky cribbed-log piers support the porte-cochere and the veranda that rests above it. The structure's asymmetrical design with protruding dormers and varied roof lines blends in perfect harmony with the landscape.

On March 1, 1872, the United States Congress decided that this landscape, this expanse of land in the far reaches of Wyoming's Northwest Territory must be preserved. The "Act of Dedication," as the Congressional bill was called, set aside "…as a public park or pleasuring ground for the benefit and enjoyment of the people" and "for the preservation, from injury or spoliation, of all timber, mineral deposits, natural curiosities, or wonders…."

AS MUCH A PART OF THE PARK AS THE GEYSER IT IS NAMED AFTER

YELLOWSTONE NATIONAL PARK, WYOMING

Tales of the volcanic craters had circulated since the 1810s. Mountain men first carried stories of a place at the head of the Yellowstone River where the earth spewed steam and mud. But few believed them.

The first official exploration of the Yellowstone region had been the 1869 Cook-Folsom-Peterson Expedition, followed the next year by the Washburn-Langford-Doane Expedition. Two surveys conducted by Ferdinand Hayden, head of the U.S. Geological Survey of the Territories, one in 1871 and another in 1872, were the first Congressionally funded expeditions.

The Hayden Survey gathered hundreds of specimens and documented the natural resources and curiosities, but it concluded that the land was of little value for anything but "recreation and geologic study." Hayden found the area too rugged and erratic for grazing, thought

Early tourist accommodations included "permanent camps" run by William W. Wylie beginning in the 1880s, where visitors arrived by stage or packhorse, below. By 1915, the luxurious inn was flourishing and private automobiles were allowed to enter Yellowstone, above.

its sparse timber stands of poor quality, and saw little future in mining there. What Hayden did find was wonder after natural wonder; the geologist was totally smitten.

When the park was created, its management was put under the Secretary of the Interior. His responsibility was to protect the miraculous, seemingly sacred land and wildlife and to make it accessible to the public. Wildlife had long made the exotic landscape home, but man used the region as well. Native peoples, including Crow, Blackfeet, Bannock, Shoshone and Nez Perce tribes, were warm-season occupants. Even after the park's formation, hunters and trappers virtually had free rein, and hunting continued until passage of the Lacey Act in 1894.

Early "pioneer tourists" usually entered the park from Montana, having been outfitted in Bozeman or Virginia City. A journey into Yellowstone was not for the faint of heart. Camping in the wilderness and running into some of the wild-looking—and sometimes -acting—mountain men, a few Indians and perhaps a thief all added to the adventure. Yet early journals portray tourists who shrugged off the discomfort, and sometime danger, for the opportunity to see the country's national treasure.

Managing the massive park was a difficult task. By 1886 the U.S. Army was put in charge, to control the souvenir-hunters, poachers, and bandits. Along with policing the park, it granted leases for construction of accommodations. Well-to-do visitors arrived by rail at the park's north entrance and transferred to horse-drawn "tally-ho" stagecoaches to continue their journeys.

"The railroad didn't get here until 1883 and, of course, that arrival of the railroad is really what kicked Yellowstone into gear," said park historian Lee Whittlesey. "All of a sudden, we had five thousand visitors that summer instead

In 1899, the acting park superintendent noted that guests needed a first class hotel in the Upper Geyser Basin to "see the greatest geysers in action." Today, visitors fill the inn's veranda to watch Old Faithful's performance.

of the five hundred to one thousand we had before that."

Primitive tent compounds provided early park accommodations. From 1883 to 1891, the Yellowstone Park Association, a subsidiary of the Northern Pacific Railway, built hotels along Yellowstone's Grand Loop Road.

Visitors, unhappy with just a side trip to Old Faithful Geyser, wanted a place to spend the night within the exotic Upper Geyser Basin. In 1884, the first lunch station/hotel, a ramshackle building aptly dubbed "the shack,"

was built. When it burned a decade later, an equally sad building replaced it. Everyone, including the acting park superintendent, seemed to want a decent hotel. In 1899, he noted in his annual report: "An opportunity to see some of the greatest geysers in action is often lost to tourists by their not being able to stay over night here."

Mismanagement and financial woes plagued the companies attempting to run the facilities, and tourists were complaining. The Northern Pacific wanted to secure its position at the park,

The Northern Pacific Railway promoted its interests in Yellowstone, which included Old Faithful Inn in the Upper Geyser Basin.

and eventually bought majority stock in the Yellowstone Park Association.

In the spring of 1901, the railroad sold its controlling stock in the Yellowstone Park Association to Harry Child, Edward W. Bach and Silas Huntley, owners of the Yellowstone Transportation Company, and Child was named president. The plan was that the new owners would work with the railroad to bring tourists to the park via the Northern Pacific line.

Train travelers were becoming more sophisticated, and demanded luxury hotels. "Initially, the middle class couldn't afford to come to a place like Yellowstone," said Leslie Quinn, who trains interpreters and guides for the inn's concessionaire. In addition to the pricey train ride, tourists were charged $50 for a five-day tour around the park, which included meals and accommodations. "That was a lot of money in those days. And it was basically well-to-do folks who could afford that, so the hotels were built to their expectations."

Child's expectations included constructing a luxury hotel at the Upper Geyser Basin. Park regulations required structures to be one-quarter mile from a natural object of interest—but officials of the Yellowstone Park Association wanted the new hotel to be closer to the area's big draw: Old Faithful Geyser.

In 1894, they got their wish when a new regulation allowed construction only one-eighth mile from the geyser. Still, it was four years before an architect designed a hotel for the site. The Department of the Interior approved A.W. Spalding's plans for a Queen Anne style hotel, but nothing happened. By 1900, frustrated Department of Interior officials were pressing for construction of a hotel.

There would be no Queen Anne hotel built next to the most famous geyser in Yellowstone National Park. Instead, Child hired Robert

Reamer. The young, self-taught architect had a very different vision. The inn's design reflects the same philosophy espoused by the Arts and Crafts Movement being embraced at that time in America. Simplicity, use of handwork and native materials, and blending the building with the site exemplified the movement's fundamental principles.

A massive gable roof dominates the original portion of the inn and, while the structure is often referred to as a giant log cabin, its skeleton is really modern frame construction of the day. Building it was a challenge, and unfortunately little of the construction work was documented. Timbers were harvested and hauled eight miles from the site, the decorative lodgepole pieces hand picked by the architect, stone quarried locally, and much of the ironwork forged on location. But chilling conditions made construction a brutal affair.

"In the winter the men had a difficult time with the nails and they would break as you hit them," said Lee Whittlesey. "So they would heat them on big stoves so that they would go into the wood more easily without shattering, because it can get quite cold here. The record is sixty six below zero."

Reamer, later known for his theater designs in Seattle, not only knew how to make the building a part of its setting, but also enjoyed high drama in his architecture. The steeply pitched roof reflects the shape of a big-top tent. Flagpoles line the widow's walk built along the peak, emphasizing that this is not merely shelter, it was a house of entertainment.

Perched in the upper reaches of the soaring lobby is a crow's nest. The trapeze-like platform that looks like a treehouse provided a venue for musicians who climbed to the crow's nest for pre- and post-dinner performances. In the early days, guests climbed through the lobby stairway

The great hall is the heartbeat of Old Faithful Inn, left, where the gnarled lodgepole pine detailing of the stairways, above, adds to its forest atmosphere.

and the suspended balconies, through the crow's nest and onto the roof for a 360-degree view of the Upper Geyser Basin. A spotlight on the widow's walk led their eyes to erupting geysers, and prowling bears attracted by garbage.

"A geyser seen in eruption under the searchlight is a most remarkable sight," a 1905 Northern Pacific Railway brochure exclaimed.

Perhaps sensitive to its unusual appearance, the Northern Pacific Railway's early "Through Wonderland" brochure explained: "The Inn is not in the least a freaky affair, pertinent to its locality. It is a thoroughly modern and artistic structure in every respect—modern in its appointments and artistic in the carrying out of an unconventional and original scheme."

"It had a rustic look to it—no doubt about that—and everyone commented on that in very, very positive terms. But the Old Faithful Inn

A lava-rock fireplace, open log-faced ceiling, and hardwood floors give the dining room the feel of a giant log cabin. A second, more refined, dining room behind the fireplace wall was completed in 1922.

Guestrooms in the Old House are the choice of purists who appreciate their original character. First floor rooms feature split log walls, left, while the upper level rooms are paneled as they were in this 1907 photograph, above.

was built as a luxury hotel," Leslie Quinn explained. "Hot and cold running water, steam heat, it was a luxury joint."

Indoor plumbing, telephones, and electricity all made it a first class hostelry. But the charm of Old Faithful Inn resides in the details.

Five hundred tons of lava rock were used to build the fireplace whose chimney tapers to a modified forty-one-foot pyramid, and features four large hearths and four smaller ones in the corners. Hanging from the chimney's face is a huge fourteen-foot wind-up clock, part of the inn's remarkable collection of ironwork.

Blacksmith George Anslie is one of the few people who have the opportunity of getting up close and personal with the clock. Perched above the floor, Anslie checks the timepiece. "It was made by George Colpitts, who was a blacksmith on the project, [and] designed by Robert Reamer. It's centuries-old technology brought into a modern setting that's still operating, that's still beautiful. It's an honor to get out here and just take a look at how the old guy made the letters and the numbers and how it was all put together."

Anslie is part of the restoration crew that keeps the inn going. He hand-forges lanterns, latchkeys, doorknockers—anything iron.

"The goal at the inn here is to make the work look like it looked originally. So my job's to try and match the texture and the color and the scale that the original architect had in mind."

Original intent lives in the dining room off the great hall—a huge log cabin with split logs covering the open, pitched roof, and lower walls.

Formally attired diners ate family-style at long tables when the inn first opened. In 1920 workers pitched a temporary canvas-roofed room to the south of the main dining room for overflow crowds. A permanent addition was completed for the 1922 season. The rooms were joined by replacing the original windows that flanked the stone fireplace with doorways. Instead of the log cabin feel of the main dining room, the annex features interior columns and beams, etched with images of park wildlife, bringing a refined touch of the outdoors inside.

The original "Old House" had 140 rooms. The first-floor rooms, with shared baths, featured rustic log decor, while the rooms on the floors above were finished with rough, un-painted pine boards. Only ten rooms had private baths. By the time the Old House was complete, Child had spent nearly $140,000 of the railway's money on the building and another $25,000 on its furnishings.

21

The inn was an immediate success and soon had to be expanded. Reamer designed and supervised construction of the east wing addition in 1913-1914, adding one hundred guestrooms at about $1,000 each. The wing's flat tar-and-gravel roof offered little competition to the Old House and its spectacular pitched roof. Redwood shingles covered the exterior walls, but the interior offered a very different atmosphere. Plaster, not wood, covered the walls. The furnishings were simple and rather austere. In 1927, Reamer designed a simple west-wing addition with 150 rooms and 95 bathrooms at a cost of over $200,000.

Today, many of those rooms are only a reminder of their "plain Jane" past. In 1992, eighty-three guestrooms and public areas in the east wing were renovated and, by 2000, one hundred twenty rooms were updated in the west wing. During renovation, the east wing was taken down to its skeleton, updated and returned to be an improved version of its original self with modern private bathrooms, and craftsman-style maple and wicker furnishings all covered in soft yellow, cream, and light green.

Still, guests who love the sense of history will stay only in the Old House, where the inclusion of sinks and new mattresses is about all that seems to have changed. Many original guestroom furnishings remain—like the brass, iron, or wood bedframes, dressers, chairs and nightstands, desks, and copper-topped wash-stands.

Back in 1933, when Prohibition had been repealed and the National Park Service lifted its ban on the sale of alcoholic drinks in the parks, celebration was warranted. The Bear Pit Cock-tail Lounge opened in what is now the inn's snack bar. Reamer thought decorative panels with sandblasted designs would liven up the space. In October 1934, he wrote the president of the Yellowstone Park Hotel Company that he would like a touch of humor added to the room: "If your Chicago cartoonist would rough out some of his funny bears they might be used to advantage."

Yellowstone's wildlife is depicted as cartoon characters in etched glass.

The result was twelve panels of dancing, hard-drinking, card-playing, party bears—along with their more refined bruin cousins—with a pair of ballroom-dancing moose and a ram waiter adding to the hilarious lineup. A successful park advertising campaign featured the bears minus libations. Today, some of the original wood panels are in the snack bar behind protective glass. In 1989, artists reproduced the panels in glass etchings that divide the main dining room wall and cocktail lounge.

Mission-style tables, davenports, rockers and settees, with rustic hickory tables and chairs, still fill the lobby and mezzanine. Oak, two-sided writing-desks with high spindle dividers and art-glass center shades—brought from the Reamer-designed Canyon Hotel after it was closed—offer the perfect place for visitors to make journal entries or write letters about the wonders just outside the door.

Montana author Gary Ferguson knows the park better than most: "People who would never write a postcard or a letter, normally, seem to be drawn to those writing tables. A lot of things about who we are, just as human beings, seem to be supported, not just by the park, but by that inn.

"When you have spent your day out in the park and you've seen the thermal features, you've seen the wild animals, you come back to the Old Faithful Inn and you're surrounded by these massive timbers, these massive stones. I think it keeps alive what you felt during that day. Yellowstone still resides every bit as much, as strongly as it did out there."

As visitors dwindle and fall snow flurries cover the terrain, Old Faithful Inn closes for its own hibernation. And each winter, nature attempts to conquer the inn.

"In the winter, this building is like a freezer," explained Barry Cantor, who has spent winters at Yellowstone since 1988 as concession operator AmFac's director of engineering. "It'll probably be fifteen or twenty below zero inside. The outside temperatures could easily be twenty-five to forty below zero."

Over the years, repairs and alterations done by people like Barry Cantor and George Anslie had kept the inn operating. "The building is different," said Cantor. "It's like a large, giant baby that every once in a while cries out and says, 'I need help,' and sometimes we're not sure what the answer is but, you know, we try to do what we can."

But by the late 1970s, time had taken a heavy toll on the grand log and frame structure.

The asymmetrical design of Old Faithful Inn—with its cribbed log piers, stone foundation and shingle roof and siding—is bathed in the setting sun's light.

Andy Beck worked as National Park Service restoration project architect for Old Faithful Inn's transformation that was done through the long winter months, left. Each fall the inn is closed for its annual hibernation, below, but not forgotten.

Rotting logs, worn shingle siding, and a deteriorating roof were the obvious problems. Inside, the lobby—once a soaring stately atrium—was shabby, its space poorly adapted, and health and safety issues needed to be addressed throughout the hotel.

A team of National Park Service architects was called upon to analyze the damage.

"There were some people that thought the Old Faithful Inn was in such bad shape we should tear it down. There were joints coming apart, the roof was collapsing in sections, logs were falling off the building," recalled NPS architect Andy Beck. "It needed a lot of work."

But Old Faithful Inn was not ready for its last gasp. Instead, a partnership with public and private funding began a ten-year, $7,350,000 restoration and rehabilitation project—a project not for the faint of heart. No federal or private log structure restoration of this scale had ever been tackled. Beck, a twenty-nine-year-old Colorado architect, became the restoration project architect.

"The Old Faithful Inn was the first big project for Robert Chambers Reamer, and it was the first big project for Andy Beck," he recalled.

In the spring of 1979 work began.

Workers started with the roof and worked their way down and through the huge wooden inn. When a log needed to be replaced, its location, shape and cuts were determined by studying historic photos. Portions of the massive inn were jacked up at the foundation in order to replace logs. Ornamental shingles were individually photographed, measured, drawn and hand-cut to the original design. Decayed gnarled-branch knee braces and lodgepole pine logs that gave the inn its character had to be replaced, along with over 1,000 squares of shingles, and hundreds of feet of logs.

Construction materials and techniques were not the only things the crew had in common with the original carpenters. Since the inn was an operating hotel, most of the work was done during its off-season. Brutal weather conditions with driving blizzards and 35°-below-zero-Fahrenheit temperatures challenged the crew, yet work was never called off due to weather. Instead, supervisors and crews devised on-site work strategies. For example, original drawings were unmanageable, particularly while roofers climbed the forty-five-degree pitch of the soaring roof, so mini-drawings were created on waterproof paper that slipped into workers' pockets.

Rehabilitation of the interior was not meant to bring the inn back to one particular time period, but rather to integrate health and safety improvements and better utilize public spaces in such a way that future additions would blend with the old.

The process also provided an opportunity to repair damaged portions of the National Historic Landmark. The stone fireplace on the south dining room wall, which had collapsed in 1959 during a 7.5-ranking earthquake, was rebuilt to its original design with a new internal steel frame. This was completed in 1988, with a historical blacksmith re-creating the firescreen. The dining room fireplace and the chimney's brick portion above the great hall were the only two notable victims of that quake or of the almost-indiscernible quakes that rumble through the park daily.

"The Old Faithful Inn gives the average visitor an opportunity to glimpse the past, to see how architecture and national parks were presented to the public almost one hundred years ago. You can reach out your hand and touch 1903," Andy Beck said as he surveyed his work.

The original carpenters built Old Faithful Inn to last fifty years. Nearly lost to fire and neglect, today it stands restored as a National Historic Landmark, a place where visitors touch the past.

The Old Faithful Inn Rehabilitation Project garnered three prestigious preservation awards: the Federal Design Achievement Award and the National Historic Preservation Award in 1992, and the President's Award for Design Excellence in 1994. Andy Beck accepted the third award from President Bill Clinton at the White House, sharing these honors with NPS architects Paul Newman and Tom Busch, who were responsible for the rehabilitation work.

"Robert Reamer taught me a lot. Perhaps he was my mentor in some ways," said Beck of his experience.

Just as the restoration team's work was completed, Robert Reamer's greatest remaining park achievement, Old Faithful Inn, was nearly lost when one of Yellowstone's stunning 1988 fires roared toward the structure. The new water system soaked the roof; volunteers stamped out sparks, then suddenly—the wind shifted. Thirty percent of the park burned, but Old Faithful Inn stood untouched.

Old Faithful Inn was the first, and some feel the finest, great lodge of the national parks. As park historian Lee Whittlesey put it: "Old Faithful Inn is as much a part of Yellowstone National Park, as the geyser it is named after."

YELLOWSTONE NATIONAL PARK

BEYOND IMAGINATION

Yellowstone National Park was the first awe-inspiring chunk of America designated as a national park. Since that day in 1872, people have roamed the remarkable landscape with the same sense of disbelief that early explorers experienced.

The power of the Lower Falls of the Yellowstone River, facing page, the brilliance of a scarlet paintbrush, right, and the formations such as Mammoth Hot Springs' Minerva Terrace, below, come together on this vast volcanic plateau.

"People come to Yellowstone for a variety of reasons," explained Gary Ferguson, whose 1993 book *Walking Down the Wild* documented his trek through Yellowstone, "but spend their hours during the day focused on one of two things. One is the geothermal features, and the second is the wildlife. Both serve as a whack on the side of the head, if you will, against the kind of insulated lives that many of us lead. You get to Yellowstone and you're seeing something you didn't quite expect and couldn't quite imagine."

The space itself is difficult to grasp. Perched on a vast volcanic plateau, Yellowstone is surrounded by mountains that include the Gallatins, Absarokas, and Beartooths. Its list of individual peaks seems as endless as the sky. Mountains reach above 11,000 feet, with meadows and range spilling across the landscape. The Continental Divide slices from northwest to southeast, and famous rivers known for their world-class trout fishing tumble through valleys and canyons before splaying across flats and grasslands.

Yellowstone's 10,000 thermal features seem otherworldly as they bubble, spew and erupt, creating more geothermal activity here than in the rest of the world combined. The twenty-five named geysers in the Upper Geyser Basin, home of Old Faithful Geyser, comprise the largest concentration of geysers on the globe. This hot spot of thermal activity exists because of the magma layer under the surface, a relatively thin two miles here. The park's volcanic history includes cataclysmic explosions that

created the twenty-eight-by-forty-seven-mile caldera that is the heart of the park.

As famous as the spewing geysers and bubbling mud pots is the wildlife. Many of the same species that made this region home 150 years ago still roam through the "wonderland," as early promotions labeled it. Bear, bighorn sheep, bison, bobcats, porcupines, beavers, coyotes, moose, elk, whitetailed and mule deer, and gray wolves—reintroduced into the park and central Idaho in 1994—are some of the fifty species of mammals. Birdlife thrives, and winged wonders like the white pelican, trumpeter swan, and sandhill crane are among the 309 species recorded in the park. The scene is rounded out with eighteen types of fish and six varieties of reptiles.

Tourists flock to the quirky geothermal sights, but some of the other treasures include 292 waterfalls careening from faces of rock. The highest and most famous, the Lower Falls of the Yellowstone River, drops 308 feet into the spectacular Grand Canyon of the Yellowstone between its various-hued rhyolite walls. Yellowstone Lake, with 110 miles of shoreline, is one of the coldest lakes in North America due to its size and 7,733-foot elevation.

Forest covers eighty percent of the park, and is home to eight species of conifers, predominantly lodgepole pine. Since the fires of 1988, there are actually more trees, albeit smaller ones, creating a landscape that only intensifies with time. Early-summer wildflower blooms paint the flats and meadows with purple lupine, white bistort, and flame-red paintbrush. Flowers change as the season progresses, offering not only beauty, but also subsistence for the wildlife that grazes the meadows. Fall colors sprinkle the landscape until winter drapes the scene in snow.

Castle Geyser in the Upper Geyser Basin attracts summer visitors, facing page, but Yellowstone takes on another personality when a spring snow dusts the landscape where bison graze, right. Gray wolves, one of Yellowstone's fifty mammal species, were reintroduced into the park in 1994, above.

Winter in Yellowstone brings a landscape that is austere but no less inspiring, and visitors can best experience it by cross-country skiing or snowshoeing through the scenery. Old Faithful Inn was built as a summer lodge and, while it is hibernating, guests at the Upper Geyser Basin stay at Old Faithful Snow Lodge, which has been open for both summer and winter seasons since 1999.

The Snow Lodge may be recent, but its design is in keeping with the Old Faithful Historic District. Other structures in that district include the Lower Hamilton Store, built in 1897

as a photo studio for F. Jay Haynes, and Old Faithful Lodge, originally a laundry built in 1918. There are more than 1,000 historic structures within the park, including Fort Yellowstone, the first buildings constructed to house the Army in 1891. Nearby the latter the steaming limestone tiers of Mammoth Terraces and the Mammoth Hot Springs Hotel, open for summer and winter seasons. Robert Reamer designed the 1935 Mammoth Springs Hotel, and was responsible for taking the historic Lake Hotel on the shores of Lake Yellowstone from dull to delightful.

And yet, even though each building is an important reminder of our past, Yellowstone's undisputed draw is nature. Annually, more than 3 million visitors wind their way over the park's 370 miles of roads or hike the 1,200 miles of backcountry trails. With each curve in the road or trail, each sighting of a bison or bear, each geothermal wonder, visitors experience what Ferdinand Hayden felt in 1871 when he wrote, "…the beholder stands amazed…at nature's handiwork."

The Ahwahnee remains the Queen of Yosemite and the most elegant lodge in the national parks, above. Gilbert Stanley Underwood's drawing shows the strong vertical core, facing page.

THE AHWAHNEE

OPENED 1927

*S*tanding in relative isolation, set in a meadow with the Royal Arches as a backdrop, and views of Half Dome, Glacier Point, and Yosemite Falls, The Ahwahnee hotel is a regal reminder of another time. A time when beauty came first, and affordability a distant second.

Two decades after the construction of Old Faithful Inn had set the tone for environmentally compatible architecture in the national parks, an unlikely group came together in Yosemite National Park. Architects, bureaucrats, businessmen, and visionaries began pooling their ideas and arguing over their differences.

The center of debate was the construction of a grand hotel in Yosemite Valley. Not meant to embody the wilds of the West as Old Faithful Inn did in Yellowstone, the plan was to construct an elegant country estate that would blend flawlessly with its remarkable setting and offer comfortable accommodations to those used to the finer things in life. The idea struck some as elitism in a public park.

But that idea was championed by Stephen T. Mather, the first director of the National Park Service. An avid outdoorsman and wealthy businessman, California native and member of the Sierra Club, Mather was recruited by Secretary of the Interior Franklin Lane to tackle

the job. Mather had hiked through most of the national parks in the West, and while he was a proponent of the parks, he complained to Lane of their poor management. Mather was indignant over the operations at Sequoia and Yosemite, and in 1914 wrote Lane. "Steve," replied the Secretary, "if you don't like the way those parks are run, you can come on down to Washington and run them yourself." Mather reluctantly decided to take the challenge, and moved to the capital where he was sworn in as Assistant to the Secretary of the Interior.

In 1916, the National Park Service was born and forty-nine-year-old Mather became its director. Horace Albright, a young University of California graduate with a degree in law, became Mather's assistant. The new director was a pragmatist who was passionate about preserving the national parks while making them accessible to tourists of every economic level. He set out with the daunting task of creating a system to manage the parks.

Mather loved the stellar beauty of Yosemite, and as NPS director, he saw an opportunity. Among his numerous challenges, here in his favorite park he envisioned a cohesive park building program for stylized structures including a grand lodge. It was Mather's belief that bringing those of wealth and influence to Yosemite and other national parks would provide future support, and thus congressional funding, to preserve them.

While the director was as comfortable in a tent in the High Sierra as in a suite at the Fairmont Hotel, he knew that most of the wealthy influential guests he wanted to woo were not.

"That meant that you needed a space where they could gather, a space that was elegant, that enhanced their experience, and exuded nature, yet fit into nature," explained Keith Walklet, whose passion for the park and hotel is reflected in his photography.

For members of the Miwok tribe, who first hunted, fished and gathered acorns in one of nature's most spectacular breadbaskets there was little need to enhance the experience. Each summer they came to the valley they called Ah-wah-ni or "large gaping mouth." The discovery of gold in the Sierra Nevada

REGAL REMINDER OF ANOTHER TIME

YOSEMITE NATIONAL PARK, CALIFORNIA

foothills, in 1849, brought a flood of miners seeking their fortunes. Conflict was not far behind. In 1851, a battalion of pioneer volunteers, in search of Indians accused of harassing miners and settlers along the lower Merced River, "discovered" the valley. Tourists infiltrated the region in 1855; in the spring of 1857 the first Yosemite hotel opened for business.

Writers, artists, and photographers spread the fame of the valley's incomparable beauty. While the nation was torn apart by the Civil War, on June 30, 1864, President Abraham Lincoln brought two relative pockets of tranquility into a protective fold. He signed a bill granting Yosemite Valley and the Mariposa Grove of Giant Sequoias to the State of California as an inalienable public trust. It was a historic move: the first time in history that a national government had set aside scenic lands simply for their protection and the enjoyment of the citizenry. It was the seed that spawned the notion of national parks.

Four years after Lincoln signed the Yosemite Grant, naturalist, conservationist and author John Muir laid eyes on Yosemite Valley. His documentation of the wonders of Yosemite caught the public's fancy. Muir and Robert Underwood Johnson, editor of *Century* magazine, were instrumental in the establishment of Yosemite National Park, finalized on October 1, 1890.

By the time Yosemite was designated a national park, tent camps, horse stables, stores, hotels, and taverns haphazardly dotted the landscape. The old Sentinel Hotel, built in 1876, was the main hostelry in the valley. The inadequacies of the hotel situation were spelled out in no uncertain terms in the State Commission's 1882 Biennial Report:

"The Yosemite Valley is preeminently the wonder of the continent. It would be for the best interests of the State, the greater comfort and satisfaction of tourists, and immeasurably to the credit of the Valley's management, if there were but one sufficient and properly appointed hotel in the premises, instead of three apologies which now respond indifferently to public want."

In 1885, California granted $40,000 for the construction of a first-class hotel. The solution was short-lived after the Stoneman burned in 1896, leaving the Sentinel Hotel again the valley's only hostelry.

By the time the National Park Service was established, private interests were entrenched at Yosemite. Mather's task was two-fold: to replace a hodgepodge of government and private buildings and upgrade the park's concession operations and accommodations. It would take the director nearly a decade for his vision of a cohesive Yosemite Village with a grand hotel to become a reality.

Mather called upon Daniel Hull, the park service's senior landscape engineer, to recommend a new site and plan for the village. By 1923, with the assistance of the Fine Arts Commission, prominent architects and landscape designers, a firm plan was approved.

Three government buildings—the post office, administration building and museum, along with the Rangers' Club—created a hub of structures that set the tone for Yosemite National Park's "rustic" design.

At the same time, Mather needed a savvy, solid company to upgrade the park's concession operations and accommodations. As with other parks, his plan was to consolidate or replace the major competing concession operators. At Yosemite, it was a particularly complex and difficult task. The history between the Yosemite Park Company and Curry Camp Company, particularly, was wrought with tense discourse.

After a decade of wrangling with the companies, on February 21, 1925, papers were signed consolidating the Curry Camp Company and Yosemite Park Company into the Yosemite Park and Curry Company (YP&CCo.). Donald Tresidder, son-in-law of Curry Company owner "Mother" Jenny Curry, was named president. Part of that contract was for the construction of a year-round, modern hotel. It was time to select an architect.

The Yosemite Village plans and construction had brought outside architects into the park. One of these was Gilbert Stanley Underwood, a friend and colleague of Hull, who was fresh from his graduate work at Harvard. In 1923,

NPS Director Stephen Mather, right, wanted a grand hotel in Yosemite, his favorite national park.

Underwood had worked briefly for the NPS and submitted plans for a post office design for the village. It was soundly rejected. Yet something in Underwood's post office plans, and his work at Zion (with Hull) impressed both Mather and YP&CCo. In July 1925, two months after Zion Lodge opened, the YP&CCo. Board of Directors hired Underwood.

With the hotel site already selected, the thirty-five-year-old architect got his marching orders. Build a first-class, "fire-proof" hotel that was in keeping with its astounding setting.

Old Faithful Inn had set a standard whereby park architecture could blend with the landscape, and the NPS's ongoing rustic style had evolved into workable and appealing designs well suited for the parks. While the Yosemite Village buildings successfully adapted the rustic ideal to larger structures, it remained for the diminutive Underwood to translate that ideal on a mammoth scale.

Underwood had dreamed of creating a large rustic hotel in his work for the Union Pacific and its Utah Parks Company. While a much smaller version of the architect's Zion Lodge (downsized by Mather) was built in 1924, it was at Yosemite where Underwood, now with the support of Mather, created The Ahwahnee.

The YP&CCo. Board of Directors hastily awarded the building contract to San Francisco contractor James L. McLaughlin. Instead of getting bids based on the architect's plans, the board, eager to begin construction, decided to forgo the bidding process—a decision all involved would regret. McLaughlin signed a contract to build the huge hotel in six months for a flat fee of $525,000.

After McLaughlin signed on, 18,000 square feet were added to the plans. McLaughlin was furious, and the board responded in kind. April 14, 1927, minutes of the Executive Committee

Meeting of the Yosemite Park and Curry Co. contain three courses of action concerning the "dispute over the Ahwahnee Hotel," ranging from dismissal of the contractor to a settlement. It was agreed that Donald Tresidder confer with McLaughlin and insist that the company "hastily complete the building" under the terms of the original contract, and upon completion of the building "an attempt would be made to settle all items in dispute." If he did not agree, McLaughlin was "to be informed to withdraw his forces from the building and to be informed that he would be sued for damages and all moneys in excess of the contract price."

Not only did the board feel McLaughlin Company was to blame, but Tresidder reported to the board that "much of the excess cost over the original estimates was due to the inefficiency and lack of knowledge on part of the architect."

But the builder and architect were players in a scenario that included the NPS and state and federal agencies. McLaughlin is credited with solving seemingly insurmountable transport and building problems. Over two hundred workers, using horses to move boulders and state-of-the-art techniques to pour the concrete forms, forged on. As the bickering and finger pointing continued, an amazing building was being erected.

Mather wanted The Ahwahnee to open on Christmas Day 1926. The idea was to have an "All-Year Hotel" built for the winter after the "All-Year Highway" (Highway 140) was completed. The highway

opened July 31, 1926, The Ahwahnee did not open until July 14, 1927.

The hotel's debut was an elegant affair, with Director Mather presiding. Finally, Mather got his grand hotel in Yosemite, his favorite national park; the YP&CCo. had a $1.5 million showpiece for its operation; and Gilbert Stanley Underwood's completed masterpiece stood as a testament to his talent.

The Mural Room features Robert Boardman Howard–painted tapestry whose subject is drawn from just outside of the window, above. With a backdrop of the towering Royal Arches, The Ahwahnee glows on a winter night, facing page.

Built predominantly of rough-cut granite, concrete, steel, and glass the building rises from the valley floor. It is an elegant yet rustic cluster of enormous blocks with two three-story wings. The core is six stories high, and each level in the asymmetrical design has a chimney, deck or porch protruding, much like the rock formations of its setting.

The vertical reliefs of the huge stone pillars meld with the similar reliefs of the surrounding cliffs. The architect's specifications stated that all stone should be "native granite and laid with the weathered surface exposed" to achieve a "rough and primitive appearance." But Underwood was a contemporary architect and also a bit ahead of his time. His use of glass is characteristic of 1930s Art Deco. Using immense glass pieces was just becoming popular. Glass created the feeling of "brightness" and "future" and at the same time brought the outdoors inside.

None of the meticulous design would have been as effective if the hotel had been placed in the middle of the meadow. Instead, Mather, his assistant Horace Albright, Secretary of the Interior Hubert Work, Donald Tresidder and YP&CCo. board members selected a site on the fringe of the meadow where a stable business called Kenneyville stood. Sheltered by ponderosa pine, black oak and sequoia trees, the hotel is almost diminished by its setting.

The details of the hotel's meadow setting—from tiny wildflowers to the valley walls—fill the soaring glass of the Solarium, above. The original hotel entry follows a long corridor where basket-weave designs are repeated in the rubber-composite tile flooring, borders, and the Basket Mural above the fireplace in the Elevator Lobby, facing page.

Underwood had signed his contract in July of 1925, and after revisions to the plans, the building finally was staked out in the spring of 1926. The positioning of the hotel with the two wings set at angles to the core emphasizes the park's magnificent wonders. The dining wing lines up with views of Yosemite Falls, while the opposite wing points toward Half Dome. Glacier Point is to the south, and individual guestroom windows frame stunning portraits of these features. Viewed from afar, The Ahwahnee seems to be anchored to the cliffs reigning high above, with proportions that are pleasing and in balance to those in the background.

The site also solved the problem of the hotel's ostentatious presence in the national park. Campers and less affluent visitors who came in droves were less likely to see the secluded hotel and be put off by the hostelry so

obviously created for the elite. And the hotel guests would not be overwhelmed by crowds of tourists.

But one major design flaw was caught only ten days prior to the opening. As delivery trucks began unloading goods, the fumes and noise rose from the original entry to guestrooms above it. A hastily constructed timber porte-cochere became the new entry. The true entrance of the building would have been what was later enclosed and is now the Indian Room cocktail lounge.

The goal of a "fire-proof" hotel was advanced, but not wholly achieved. Slate replaced the shingle roof called for in Underwood's specifications, and only the roof framing and exterior logs in the Dining Room and some balconies are wood. Underwood called for siding and beams made of concrete, both poured into timber molds, then stained to look like redwood. End beams

have rings, boards reflect the wood grain, and the effect is remarkable. But molds were reused, and a close viewing unveils the repetition of the wood-grain design.

Dr. Arthur Pope, a Persian arts expert, and his wife, Dr. Phyllis Ackerman, a tapestry authority, were commissioned to decorate and furnish the hotel. The University of California at Berkeley academic and his one-time student moved to the valley to tackle the job. It was a brilliant selection. The two set about transforming the massive public spaces and one hundred guest rooms into lush, warm rooms in keeping with the board's desire that the hotel's atmosphere should be that of a "country home."

The team was acutely aware of just whose "country" the Yosemite Valley had belonged to. While their art history backgrounds were rooted in the Near and Middle East, the couple's interest was with indigenous peoples and the crafts they created. Pope and Ackerman turned to the motifs and patterns found in the basketry of the California Indians as the basis of their entire design.

The geometric patterns found in the original basketry were interpreted on the ceiling beams, stained glass windows, rubber mosaic tiles, concrete floors, and multiple borders, reinforcing the true roots of The Ahwahnee.

Guests enter the lobby from the sugar-pine log porte-cochere. To the left is the Indian Room cocktail lounge, the doomed entry. From this point guests can see Underwood's original introduction to the hotel: a long corridor with mosaic floors, huge pillars, floor-to-ceiling windows facing the meadow, and a registration desk tucked to the right. The mosaics, an ancient form usually done in marble, glass or ceramic, utilize a contemporary material, rubber tile, set within outlines of brass wire. At the end of the hallway of the Main Lobby is the fireplace of the Elevator Lobby.

The Elevator Lobby is a buffer between The Ahwahnee's two most magnificent rooms: the Great Lounge and the Dining Room. Above the Lobby fireplace is Jeannette Dyer Spencer's famous mural, a swirl of basket patterns carefully laid one upon the other.

Nearly hidden behind the fireplace wall rises the cathedral-like Great Lounge that matches the majesty of Yosemite. Rich, warm golden walls, wood floors, and heavy upholstered furniture soften its massive size. As on the valley floor outside, one's eyes immediately gaze up to take in the entire scene. Two walls are banked with floor-to-ceiling windows, and atop each huge vertical span of glass are five-by-six-foot stained-glass panels that again interpret the Indian basket motif. Created by Spencer, the stained-glass windows were not originally planned, rather included when the decorators disliked the original design.

The furniture, chosen for comfort, solidity and proportion, was borrowed from various periods. The massive 17th century tables are English, but the benches from the same era are American design, as are the secretaries placed between each window. The chandeliers may reflect German Gothic workmanship, but the detail is again California Indian design.

Kilim, soumak and other Middle Eastern rugs were purchased in bulk and used on the floors and walls. Like the basketry, they were made by nomadic people with parallel cultural backgrounds. The collection, recognized today as museum quality, is displayed on walls throughout The Ahwahnee. Two enormous fireplaces of cut sandstone define each end of the room.

The hotel seems never to end, and past the Great Lounge are four more rooms. The half-circle Solarium of two-story windows extends off the end of the building. Here the architect and decorators knew nothing could compete

The cathedral-like Great Lounge matches the majesty of Yosemite Valley. Warm golden walls, wood floors, and heavy upholstered furniture soften its massive size.

with nature. The floor-to-ceiling windows welcome the towering views of Glacier Point and the graceful details of the meadow with flowers, trees, and even roaming animals. Water from the jasper rock fountain softly trickles in the background.

The Stairway Lounge offers access to The Mural and Winter Club rooms and the mezzanine. The Mural Room, originally the writing room, features the famous Robert Boardman Howard toile peinte mural. This painted tapestry draws from the valley, with a profusion of flowers, birds, and animals. It, along with the wood paneling and hammered copper corner fireplace, reflects the Arts and Crafts movement begun in England by William Morris. The Winter Club Room is now filled with park memorabilia, and a Christmas tree fills the window frame each December.

Upstairs, one can gaze from the Tudor Lounge onto the Great Lounge. Two additional rooms flanking the Tudor Lounge are used for conference and party needs.

The natural elegance of Underwood's interior is the perfect backdrop for the exquisite decor and artwork. The decorators complemented Underwood's massive elements with the smallest detail. The constant contrasts of large and small—huge pillars and fireplaces with delicate stencil work or grand spaces next to cozy sitting rooms and lounges—show that both the architect and decorators followed the natural surroundings where granite cliffs share the landscape with tiny wild flowers. From every room one "sees" Yosemite.

The room that most "says" Yosemite to longtime visitors is the Dining Room. If guests and staff were polled, the Dining Room would likely be voted "most popular." Its success is also a departure from the country home feel of the hotel. A bow to the traditional "lodge"

design of other national park lodges is found in the 6,630-square-foot room. Sugar-pine roof trusses—an Underwood trademark—cradle the roofline. The same pine logs line the north and south walls, but each has a steel core to help support the structure. Pine columns alternate with floor-to-ceiling windows facing the meadow. Stone columns at the far end of the room frame an alcove and another soaring window offering up a view of one of Yosemite's great treasures—Yosemite Falls. Geometric Indian designs decorate the gable and are painted between the roofline and the windows. Scored and acid stained concrete covers the floor.

The YP&CCo. began promoting Yosemite's grand hotel as the much-awaited all-year lodge ready to "cater to influential people who had ceased coming to Yosemite owing to the crowds" knowing that it would never be a substantial earnings source for the company. But there were other perks.

In addition to the social elite, celebrities, politicians, and royalty began coming to the hotel. In 1927, future President Herbert Hoover was a guest, and in the years to follow, Franklin and Eleanor Roosevelt, Winston Churchill, Dwight Eisenhower, John Kennedy, and Ronald Reagan joined the rooster of important dignitaries. In March of 1983 Queen Elizabeth and Prince Philip visited Yosemite and took over the entire hotel.

Hollywood filmed on location in Yosemite, and guests at The Ahwahnee included Desi Arnaz and Lucille Ball, Judy Garland, Shirley Temple, Helen Hayes, Jack Benny and Red Skelton, to name a few.

Ansel Adams became an integral part of the hotel. Besides his photographic work for the YP&CCo., and his growing reputation as a landscape photographer, Adams was an accom-

Each Christmas, The Ahwahnee's Dining Room is transformed into an English manor for the annual Bracebridge Dinner.

plished pianist. His impromptu afternoon recitals on the hotel's Steinway grand piano drew crowds that prompted hotel personnel to begin afternoon tea in the Great Lounge. It's a tradition that continues today.

In 1928, another tradition was born when the first Bracebridge Dinner was hosted. It was to be the ultimate Christmas dinner party. What transpired could have only happened at The Ahwahnee. Based on Washington Irving's "Sketch Book" of a Christmas Day in 1718 at Squire Bracebridge's Old English Manor, the dinner is both a musical pageant and a feast.

The hugely popular event is part of The Ahwahnee's history. A young Ansel Adams played the court jester in the early days; he and Jeannette Dyer Spencer soon ran the show. The Dining Room is transformed into an 18th century English estate where a seven-course feast is served to the accompaniment of music that fills the hall and hearts of every guest. Demand for the Bracebridge Dinner today stretches it to a five-night affair, with a total of 1,675 tickets offered on a lottery basis.

In 1934, Adams asked Eugene Fulton, a Bay Area choral conductor, to lead the eight-member male chorus. Adams retired from his Bracebridge duties in 1973, and Eugene and his wife Anne-Marie Fulton became musical directors and continued until Eugene's sudden death on Christmas Eve 1978. Today, their daughter Andrea Fulton recreates the spectacle her family cherished.

As Andrea prepared for her fiftieth year as a Bracebridge regular in December 2000, she explained its charm: "The Bracebridge represents a Christmas that never was but a Christmas that lives in everyone's heart. The essence of the Bracebridge dinner is capturing the beauty of music, nature and pageantry and combining them to give the guest a truly spiritual experience."

The formal feast and all other meals are prepared in the 6,500-square-foot kitchen. Until lack of a federal budget briefly closed all parks

During WWII the elegant Tressider Suite was used for Navy officer housing.

in 1995, only floods and World War II caused the cancellation of a Bracebridge Dinner.

World War II also prompted the remarkable transformation of the elegant building into a military installation. On May 30, 1943, The Ahwahnee closed its doors as a civilian hotel, and on June 7, 1943, the U.S. Navy took charge of it as a convalescent hospital. Most of the valuable furniture and artwork was inventoried and shipped to storage facilities in Oakland, California.

The commanding officers got the sixth-floor Tresidder suite, nurses occupied the fifth floor, and the Great Lounge was converted into a dormitory for 350 men. Other rooms and wings were used for wards, labs and X-ray machines, and El Dorado Diggin's Bar (once in the mezzanine above the Dining Room) was converted into a chapel. At times, up to 853 patients plus staff filled the hotel, cabins and surrounding buildings, and few were happy with their remote location in the Yosemite Valley.

When the Navy moved out, staff returned and began an almost $400,000 restoration of the building and furnishings that included everything from fumigation to reupholstering furniture. Besides the building, the grounds, designed by Frederick Law Olmsted, Jr., were ruined. YP&CCo. later sued the government for damages. The hotel was brought back to its glory days.

The National Park Service manages Yosemite, a 761,266-acre piece of paradise, with Yosemite Concession Services Corporation (YCS) directing guest services since 1993, but the ultimate boss is Mother Nature. Rockslides close roads and campgrounds, fires change habitats, and three major floods have transformed the valley. In January of 1997, the Merced River overflowed its banks, and the flood waters that ravaged the park left nature's calling card: roads and bridges buried under debris, hiking trails destroyed, fallen trees, uprooted flora, and nearly 400 rooms eliminated from Yosemite Concession Services' guestroom inventory.

Yet, The Ahwahnee was untouched. A bit of good luck, since $1.5 million was being spent refurbishing and redecorating the hotel including the hotel guest rooms and twenty-four cottage rooms.

A National Historic Landmark, it remains today simply the most elegant hostelry in the national parks.

Those who visit Yosemite rarely leave untouched. People like Julie Miller, a former park ranger who leads Twilight Tours from the hotel, see it each day. "Certain places heal us, they encourage us, inspire us, they fill us with a sense of awe and wonder that we don't get when we go to other places. For some people it is Yosemite, for some people it is The Ahwahnee hotel," she says as her eyes scan the meadow from the hotel terrace. "I think there's a certain feeling that you get no other place than when you're right here."

The room that most "says" Yosemite to longtime Ahwahnee guests is the Dining Room.

YOSEMITE NATIONAL PARK

NATURE'S TEMPLE

Before motor travel to Yosemite National Park, the trip from San Francisco took two full days. Today, in a few hours you can drive from the sprawl of urban life to this oasis. The most majestic entrance is through the western gate, where your introduction begins as you travel beneath the cool granite of Arch Rock—then suddenly, the valley lies before you. Naturalist John Muir described it best in 1912:

"The walls are made up of rocks, mountains in size, partly separated from each other by side cañons, and they are so sheer in front, and so compactly and harmoniously arranged on a level floor, that this Valley, comprehensively seen, looks like an immense hall or temple lighted from above.

"But no temple made with hands can compare with Yosemite. Every rock in its walls seems to glow with life."

Those temple walls include Cathedral Rocks and El Capitan. In front of you looms Half Dome, an 8,842-feet-high chunk of granite that defines the valley. The cliffs are some of the world's most famous climbing faces, and if Muir were alive today, he might say they "glow with life" in a very different way. One of the evening's eeriest sights is to watch the lights of hanging campers on the sheer face of El Capitan as they bed down for the night.

The massive seven-mile valley swath was created as glaciers carved through the canyon of the Merced River. Your eyes shift from the huge jutting walls to the blankets of tiny wildflowers that cover meadows, then on to oak woodlands that blend with forests of feathery cedar and towering ponderosa and Douglas-fir trees.

And the sound of water! Yosemite, Bridalveil, Vernal, Nevada, and Illilouette falls tumble off the granite walls until the dry months of late summer and early fall, when their only reminder often is the water imprint worn on the

"When people look at photographs of Yosemite they don't think it can be real," said photographer Keith Walklet. Yet it is. Bridalveil Fall with the Merced River, facing page, El Capitan on a winter morning, right, and Vernal Fall rushing with spring water, below, illustrate the seasons of the Yosemite Valley.

A double rainbow arcs over Yosemite Valley, above, and Half Dome peeks above clouds of swirling mist in front of the sheer face of El Capitan from Tunnel View on a morning following a heavy rain.

cliffs. Sandy beaches bank the Merced River, and you can simply wallow in the magnificence of it all.

"Each feature—El Capitan, Half Dome, Yosemite Falls—they would all qualify as a national park in their own right and yet here in Yosemite, in Yosemite Valley in particular, they're concentrated in one place. It's incredible," photographer Keith Walklet explained as he hiked a trail, tripod and camera in hand.

The valley is best experienced on foot, and hiking trails seem everywhere. If you can't hike, bicycles, horses and open-air shuttle buses give an opportunity to take in the beauty of the park. Glacier Point, thirty-two miles from the valley floor, is one of Yosemite's most famous vistas. From its 7,200 feet in elevation, the valley's panorama unfolds 3,000 feet below—to the amazement of everyone who takes the visual plunge.

Dick Ewart watches those faces every day. A park ranger for nearly thirty years, most of that time at Yosemite, he lives at Glacier Point during the summer, and gives interpretive talks. "It's great to work [here] because you get to see

people coming out here for the very first time. It's like their first experience ever and you get to see it day after day. And people are just in awe. They just stand there and look out and just can't believe what they're looking at, because they're looking at a third of Yosemite."

This love affair has taken its toll on the park, and the meadows, riverbanks, and oak woodlands have been damaged by long-term human uses, so you are asked to respect the restoration efforts and to stay within designated areas.

The park's natural wonders are also filled with cultural history found at the Yosemite Museum and Indian Village, Ansel Adams Center, homesteaders' cemetery, and apple orchard that now are along a pedestrian promenade in the heart of the village. Historic buildings and bridges blend with the valley's landscape.

Nearly four million people visit the park each year. Seventy percent of the visitors spend their time in Yosemite Valley, but the 1,169-square-mile park encompasses much more, and ninety-four percent of that is wilderness.

You will have two very different experiences

visiting Tuolumne Meadows on the park's eastern boundary–at an elevation of 8,575 feet the largest subalpine meadow in the Sierra–and the Mariposa Grove of Giant Sequoias, where 500 of the towering trees survive in the southern portion of the park. Visitors arriving through the south entrance can enjoy another National Landmark at the Wawona Hotel, built in 1879. The golf course, built in 1917, and Wawona's Pioneer Yosemite History Center are parts of the historic district.

Unlike many mountain national parks that virtually go into hibernation with the winter storms, Yosemite simply shifts gears. The Yosemite Winter Club was established in 1928 to encourage the development of winter sports. Badger Pass, site of one of the West's first mechanical ski lifts, is a fifty-minute drive from the valley. Two backcountry winter ski huts offer refuge for cross-country skiers and snowshoers.

The valley is chock-full of snow-flocked delights. There is nothing to compare to the sight of the great waterfalls breaking from their cloaks of ice and dropping to the snow-covered land-scape below.

Eighty species of mammals, including mule deer and black bears, call the park home. Once-scarce peregrine falcons are among the 247 types of birds; twenty-four different reptile and am-phibian species are all protected within park boundaries.

Yosemite National Park was designated a World Heritage Site on October 31, 1984, and its stewardship falls into the hands of people, who must care for both its natural and cultural history. Those histories come together most gracefully in the meadow of Yosemite Valley, where The Ahwahnee hotel, built in concert with its setting, stands as a reminder that beauty created by man can stand in unity with its natural surroundings.

Most visitors spend their time in the valley, but scenes like Sawtooth Ridge can be found in the park's high country.

PACIFIC NORTHWEST

The volcanic Cascade Range brims with natural and man-made wonders: Paradise Inn in the shadow of Mount Rainier; Timberline Lodge 6,000 feet up the face of Mount Hood; and Crater Lake Lodge on the rim of Mount Mazama's gigantic caldera. Along with Oregon Caves Chateau tucked into the Siskiyou Range, each thrives because people of the Northwest care.

Paradise Inn seems dwarfed by the dome of Mount Rainier, above. Ongoing work to reinforce the inn includes creating new architectural drawings, facing page.

PARADISE INN

OPENED 1917

Sandwiched between Puget Sound and the Cascade Range, Seattle may be a metropolitan jewel of the Pacific Northwest, but Mount Rainier is its touchstone. With the glaciated dome of the stratovolcano rising 14,410 feet above the lush Washington forests, it is the heart of the park that bears its name.

An icon of the Northwest, as park superintendent Jon Jarvis called it. When the sun is shining and the clouds have lifted, it is the region's best known beacon, seen from hundreds of miles away.

"It's certainly a great lump of a mountain. A beautiful white cupcake sitting over there on the horizon," commented Ruth Kirk, as she hiked along a park trail just as she has for half a century. "Rainier is really fundamental to our sense of place here in the northwest."

Nestled in the Paradise Valley at the foot of Rainier is a log and shingle reminder that man can venture into such dramatic beauty and leave a gentle mark.

"Paradise Inn is an opportunity for the public to come here and slow down and experience a little bit of the Old World," said Superintendent Jarvis of the inn that stands much as it did in 1917. "It's integral to the experience of Paradise. If it were anywhere else it just wouldn't have the sense of place. But the Paradise Inn and the meadows of Paradise and the views of the mountain all are just intertwined, and it creates an experience that is unforgettable."

On March 2, 1999, Mount Rainier National Park celebrated its centennial. The notion of protecting the region formally began in 1893, when President Benjamin Harrison set aside forty-square miles as the Pacific Forest Reserve,

with the mountain anchoring it. In 1897 Congress expanded the site and changed its name to Mount Rainier Forest Reserve, but that status would not protect the scenic and scientific wonders of the area. What was needed was national park designation.

Interest in establishing a park was shared by scientists, conservationists, mountaineers and scholars, along with Seattle and Tacoma businessmen and the Northern Pacific Railway. Academics and conservationists focused on the unique geography and geology of the active volcano (it erupted with clouds of steam and ash in the 1840s, and had undocumented activity in 1894) with its massive glaciers, crevices, cascading falls, fields of wild flowers, and wildlife. Business interests looked at the park in terms of tourism and drawing commerce to the Puget Sound.

Politicians weighed in, and when all was said and done, Congress, under President William McKinley, created Mount Rainier National Park. Since that day in March 1899, the park has been a work in progress.

That one-hundred-year progress is only a blip on Mount Rainier's geologic screen. The mountain originally stood 16,000 feet, but was cut down to size about 6,000 years ago when an eruption caused the summit to collapse. That eruption left a sixty-mile-long mudflow to Puget Sound in its wake. Earthquakes, erosion, and geothermal activity have created what stands today, and 100,000 people now live on land that was once buried by giant flows the mountain spewed over the past 10,000 years.

The Nisqually, Yakama, Cowlitz, Muckleshoot and Puyallup Indian tribes were among those to live in the shadow of the moun-

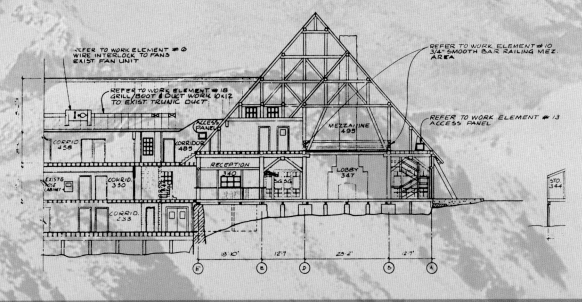

GENTLE MARK AGAINST A MAJESTIC MOUNTAIN
MOUNT RAINIER NATIONAL PARK, WASHINGTON

The first director of the National Park Service, Stephen T. Mather, far right, helped plan facilities to enhance visitors' experiences; a great lodge in Paradise Valley was on his list. Workers built the inn of local timber harvested from a burn area called the Silver Forest, below.

tain that many native peoples called Takhoma. Captain George Vancouver first spotted the peak while sailing Puget Sound in 1792, and he named the mountain after Royal British Naval Admiral Peter Rainier.

The local tribes believed that spirits lived in the summit, and they kept their distance from the crater. But white explorers and settlers longed to see for themselves. Hazard Stevens and Philemon Van Trump were the first mountaineers to reach the summit in 1870.

In 1888, naturalist John Muir visited Rainier and called the Paradise Valley "…the most extravagantly beautiful of all the alpine gardens I ever beheld in all my mountain-top wanderings." That same year, explorer and guide James Longmire laid claim to twenty acres around a hot springs seven miles east of what is now the Nisqually park entrance, and built a small cabin that stands today. He constructed a hotel and tent cabins, promoted the hot springs into healing baths, and built a toll road. In the early 1900s work began on construction of a road

from the park entrance to Paradise. The job was completed in 1915 just as the National Park Service was established.

The NPS was struggling for its stamp of congressional approval when Stephen T. Mather, assistant to the Secretary of the Interior and future director of the NPS, visited here in July 1915. Mather had climbed Mount Rainier for the first time in 1905, so he appreciated the peak's grandeur. A decade later, the visit was not a mountaineering expedition, but part of a sweeping trip of the parks taken by him, his assistant Horace Albright, and a rotating group of influential men, to promote the National Park Service and address its role within the park.

In other parks, railroad money backed development, but in the Pacific Northwest the railroads couldn't make the grade up to the high mountain areas. These parks were developed with less railroad intervention and consequently less capital for public accommodations. The job would have to be done on the local level.

Mather was dismayed at the carnival atmosphere of competing concessionaires, and he dreamed of a seamless park experience.

The new superintendent brought together a group of Tacoma and Seattle businessmen and, while on an eighty-five-mile pack trip around the mountain, Mather began the campaign to form the Rainier National Park Company.

"They did a tour around the park, and then went back to Rainier Club in Seattle, and he laid the cards on the table," said Laurin Huffman, a NPS historical architect. "He dangled in front of them the fact that if Seattle and Tacoma did not pull together an organization to consolidate the services in the park, he would bring outside capital (eastern capital was the word they used back then) to accomplish the same thing."

Besides more cohesive management and upgrading existing facilities, Mather wanted a great lodge in the Paradise Valley with views of Mount Rainier and the Tatoosh Range.

The idea of a luxury hotel in the park was not new. In 1911, Tacoma architect Frederick Heath proposed a $2 million "dream project" for a 400-room hotel featuring a glass observatory, four wings, a sanitarium, natatorium, club house, tennis courts, gardens, and its own power plant—to be built near the park's entrance at Longmire, with access to the natural mineral springs. The plans were presented to the Tacoma Commercial Club and Chamber of Commerce, where Commercial Club manager T.H. Martin began drumming up

support from a skeptical audience.

The idea languished, but apparently not Martin's enthusiasm. On March 1, 1916, a charter for incorporation was taken out, and T.H. Martin was made general manager of Rainier National Park Company.

The Nisqually Entrance Gateway was constructed in 1911 from logs selected with the same proportion and character as trees of the surrounding forest.

The company eventually bought out both the National Park Inn and Longmire Springs Hotel operations at Longmire, and John Reese's tent camp operation at Paradise. As the Rainier National Park Company took shape, new

architectural drawings were being done by Heath & Gove. By the summer of 1915, Frederick Heath's initial "dream" plan had been scaled down and the site moved to Paradise Valley. John Reese initially agreed to build a $40,000 hotel at his tent camp, but National Park officials wanted Reese out of the picture. Reese balked at initial hotel plans, saying the structure not only would cost from $350,000 to $400,000, but also was not suited to the site and snow conditions. Mr. Reese was no match for Stephen Mather and was being edged out of the Mount Rainier National Park concession operations.

Drawings and stories of the proposed Paradise Inn ran in the Tacoma newspapers on February 13, 1916. On March 28, Frederick Heath officially unveiled drawings to the Board of Directors of the two-week-old Rainier National Park Company. The newspaper illustration showed a three-winged building with a cylindrical center topped by a cone-shaped roof. The inn would have a great hall with a two-and-a-half-story ceiling and an equally large dining room. Guestrooms would be above the dining room with a kitchen wing to the north. A three-story wing on the east side and one on the south side would have additional guestrooms, baths, and suites. The majority of guests would be housed in bungalow tents on the grounds.

By this time, the philosophy was that instead of evoking a feeling of "conquering the wilder-

The log framing and stone fireplace of the great hall have always reflected the natural features of the park, above. Part of the inn's charm is the hand-crafted furniture such as the grandfather clock, facing page.

ness," parks were to preserve it. The design principles of Andrew Jackson Downing and Frederick Law Olmsted were being adapted in the parks to express their natural features and elements.

For Paradise Inn, native material would be used, including cedar shingles and native rock masonry. An 1885 fire provided the inn's most distinctive material. Weathered timbers from a burn area known as the Silver Forest on the slopes of Mount Rainier were salvaged and used for construction.

"The structural elements of the interior and exterior in their native form express the natural features of the park," explained Laurin Huffman. "We have timbers inside that represent the trees right here at timberline. Massive stone fireplaces that came from the mountain represent the massive geological elements."

Those elements especially come together when Mount Rainier is camouflaged in cloud cover, or rain and snow obscure any views.

People like Laurin Huffman see beyond the weather: "On days when you can't see the mountain, you get an experience of being in the forest and seeing the stones of the mountain in the fireplace. It brings the outdoors in and you don't leave it."

Paradise Inn went up quickly during the summer and fall of 1916. Material had been stockpiled, and while the new road to the valley was not open until late August, foundation work still began on July 20. Workers set the naturally weathered Alaska-cedar logs in a rock foundation, creating a post and beam frame. Cedar shingles cover the exterior, and the original plan was to let them weather to match the Silver Forest cedar timbers and to paint the roof. The company's proposal for a red roof was vetoed by National Park Service landscape architect Charles Punchard, and it was painted dark green. A three-level guest wing was added on the east side soon after the main building was completed, and most guests shared bathrooms.

The inn opened on schedule—July 1, 1917—having cost $100,000, and tourists were lining up to stay the night. Snow-clogged roads didn't stop guests, who boarded sleighs or horses to make their way to the valley. Others buckled on snowshoes, and waterproof boots were made available for men and women who wanted to hike in.

Their reward was much the same experience that awaits guests today: a chance to lounge in the 50-by-112-foot great hall in front of one of two massive fireplaces, take their meals in the equally impressive dining room, then adjourn to simple sleeping quarters.

That experience is now in the hands of people like James "Rusty" Sproatt, who has been managing director for Mount Rainier Guest Services since the spring of 1991. "Everybody has a perception when they come to these types of facilities. [They] were built for, not necessarily as hotels, but more of a place to rest during the evening and spend your daytime out in the park. The inn is not full of modern conveniences—telephones, TVs—we don't have 'em."

To most, like Ruth Kirk, the lack of amenities adds to its charm: "I'm not sure television would really enhance your experience of the mountain. You might be tempted to stay in and watch some sitcom instead of watching the sunset."

Over the years, alterations and decorative painting have changed some of the detail of the great hall, but it retains the grandeur of its early days. Light streams in from the dormer windows high above the mezzanine, highlighting the repetitive structural framework with posts, beams and trusses that mark the architectural signature of the great hall. Iron rungs grip the cedar poles, added to reinforce the splitting timbers, and a system of cables and metal bracing helps support the building against the onslaught of heavy snow. During the 1920s, additional cedar beams were added to create a permanent brace against the snow.

Alaska-cedar-shaped andirons hold burning

logs in the four-by-six-foot fireplaces made from locally quarried stone. Hand-painted forest and icicle designs, done sometime in the 1930s, decorate the huge cedar poles. Inn manager Paul Sceva added the mezzanine that circles the great hall from the second-floor level.

"The mezzanine in the great hall of this wonderful building was added primarily for structural support. The building itself is trying to resist immense world-record snowfalls that we get up here at Paradise," explained NPS historical architect Vicky Jacobson.

The mezzanine is an ideal getaway spot to read, write, or drink tea while observing the goings-on below. Natural light pours through the dormers and hickory tables and chairs—many originals—fill the space. It is also a good place to get a close look at the joinery work. According to Sceva's memoirs, these were originally hand-notched; snow loads that were slowly crushing the huge structure required the addition of bolts and bracing.

The Japanese lanterns and rustic triangular log fixtures that originally hung from the ceiling were replaced in the 1930s by lights with parchment shades decorated with paintings of wild flowers done by wives of park employees and women from nearby villages. Eventually, the paper shades began to disintegrate.

In 1989, Dale C. Thompson, a retired park naturalist and wildlife artist, painted the current conical shades with such themes as "bunchberry dogwood," "monarch butterfly," and "alpine autumn." Thompson used the same heavy tag board and raffia lacing that the old shades were made of and created the delicate flowers with "good old children's tempera." There are seventy-four shades in five sizes. Above the floral lights are original cone-shaped light fixtures hanging like so many belfry bats. For Thompson, what is most gratifying is knowing

"that the lampshades that I painted for the inn may be here for another fifty years."

The inn's first batch of furniture was salvaged from the Stratford Hotel in Tacoma, scheduled for demolition and owned by a member of the Rainier National Park Company Board of Directors. The board got a "deal" on the Arts and Crafts style furniture, but the inn deserved furnishings more in keeping with its setting.

Distinctive and unusual furniture began to appear in the inn after the first season. Hans Fraehnke, a German-born local carpenter, took on the task of creating furniture from local materials. "He started coming up here for seven years crafting furniture from the local Alaska-cedar. He trudged up in the spring when the snows relented and spent all summer until probably around November when he was chased out by the weather," explained Vicky Jacobson.

Massive Alaska-cedar split-log tables with matching benches were followed by a pair of throne chairs. If Fraehnke wasn't building furniture, he was customizing anything ordinary at the inn. He covered the front and sides of the registration desk with cedar, put cedar posts with triangular wood caps between the clerk's windows and designed the mailbox to look like a log stump. Fraehnke's most interesting transformation was turning a standard upright piano into a rustic piece of art. It was at this piano that President Harry Truman played a few tunes during a surprise 1945 visit.

Perhaps the most impressive of Fraehnke's designs is the fourteen-foot-tall grandfather clock presiding over the Paradise Inn great hall. The clock, made in three sections, is topped with whittled post points, as are the piano and some of the throne chairs.

Beautiful hickory chairs, tables, and settees

Andirons shaped like Alaskan cedar trees, above left, fill the fireplace openings. Rustic cedar "throne" chairs, left, and an upright piano, once played by President Harry Truman, above, were designed by Hans Fraehnke.

Facing page: The 50-by-112-foot great hall, with its repetitive post and beam design, has had structural supports and a mezzanine added, but seems as grand as the day it opened.

from the Old Hickory Company of Indiana accompanied Fraehnke's cedar furnishings. Although the Stratford Hotel furniture was replaced, the massive cedar furniture and many of the original hickory pieces remain in Paradise Inn. Much of the original furniture at other great lodges disappeared over time; perhaps Hans Fraehnke built his pieces not only to last, but to stay put. The huge tables weigh 1,500 pounds, and it is unlikely that the throne chairs (from five to six feet high) would fit anywhere else.

As architect Huffman put it: "The combination of the soaring roofline, oversized furniture—you felt like one of the Seven Dwarfs entering Fantasyland because you became small in relation to the elements of the building. That made you think that you were just one little piece in the big wheel of life, and your place in the natural order."

If man can define "natural order" at Paradise Inn, it is best found in the dining room. The feel of the room has changed little since the first guests broke bread there. Diners enter through French doors from the great hall, and walk down four steps into the one-and-one-half-story, 51-by-105-foot room. Tables and chairs are arranged diagonally as they were in the 1920s. The dining room may have nearly the same floor space as the great hall, but it, along with the kitchen, is set back from the great hall wing with a slightly lower roofline. Exposed log timbers with beams and trusses add to the room's interest. A fifty-foot-high stone fireplace fills the north wall. Windows bank the length of the room. The triangular log light fixtures are original, perhaps moved from the great hall. Reproductions of the wild-flower lanterns hang along the side.

In 1920, with guests demanding more than the tent cabins that surrounded the inn, the four-story Paradise Annex was built. Designed by

Rainier National Park Company architect Harlan Thomas, the annex featured one hundred rooms, fifty-eight with private baths. Had the Heath & Gove original plans with a cylindrical hub been executed, the annex would have been accessed off the hub. Instead, only one wing was built and the annex originally stood alone. A later addition of a three-level "tunnel" or

Wildlife artist Dale C. Thompson painted the parchment shades with native wildflower designs.

breezeway from the east wing connected the annex to the main building. Exposed log framing was proposed for the exterior, but never added.

The additions to Paradise Inn thrilled the traveling public, which increased with the end of World War I. The Milwaukee Railway dropped guests off in Ashford, where Rainier National Park Company (RNP Co.) hired fourteen buses to shuttle them into the park. By 1924, all park visitation and RNP Co. records

had been broken. The company was making a profit; the combined guest count for Paradise Inn, National Park Inn, and the cabins reached 1,500 each weekend, according to park files.

Tent cabins were taken down and housekeeping cabins constructed. The company installed water in the main rooms, refurnished the guestrooms in the annex and hoped for the best. In 1931, they even built a golf course. The concessionaire also promoted skiing. Ski competitions, carnivals, and tournaments were held during the 1930s, and in 1936-1937, the company opened the inn for the winter season. A portable ski tow was installed.

Many of the changes at Paradise Inn came while Paul Sceva, who managed and promoted Paradise Inn for forty-six years, was in charge. Sceva suggested replacing most of the original peaked and gabled dormers—ruined by snow loads—with shed dormers. In 1935, he also recommended demolishing and replacing the original kitchen and adding the gift shop on the west side of the lobby, plus enlarging the lobby porch. Sceva sold the housekeeping cabins around the inn, and in the end, lobbied on behalf of RNP Co. for the government to buy the company's holdings.

World War II brought a decline in visitors to Mount Rainier. The inn continued operation under rationing regulations and with a small staff through the war years. In 1942-1943, the U.S. Army used the facilities for troops testing mountain travel, food and equipment, and training for winter mountain conditions. After the war, the park service inventoried and appraised the buildings at Paradise. Time and winter had taken their toll. The failing Rainier National Park Company sold Paradise Inn to the National Park Service in 1952, and the park service, in turn, contracted with concessionaires to operate the inn.

In the 1960s, the National Park Service proposed demolishing the inn. Public uproar was immediate. In response, the NPS budgeted $1.75 million to restore the inn in 1979. Major rehabilitation, including a lateral restraint system, new floor systems, and repair to the roofs and windows, occurred but additional rehabilitation requires congressional funding. Additional interior steel beams reinforce some of the exterior log columns. The inn was spruced up for the 1999 centennial celebration with new paint and roof shingles.

The post, beam and truss structure with the pitched gable roof was meant to withstand the tons of snow that buried the building each winter. Unfortunately, the tremendous lateral crush of snow and ice on the uphill side of the building play havoc with the design. For eighty-five years, engineers, architects and contractors have been trying to reinforce the structure.

Caring for a national landmark is an endless responsibility, and the NPS and private concessionaires share the task. But it is a job with sometimes intangible benefits.

In this modern age, Paradise Inn's rustic charm still endures. An historic time capsule from another era, it still entices visitors with its simple, rugged elegance.

"I think the inn has charm—an appeal to us, partly because it is old. Something that is old is familiar. It is the same building our parents and grandparents saw. That has great appeal," added Kirk of this historic piece of architecture.

Mount Rainier National Park celebrated its centennial in 1999, when Paradise Inn got a fresh coat of paint, and worn cedar shingles were replaced.

MOUNT RAINIER NATIONAL PARK

AN ICON OF THE NORTHWEST

The highest and most massive peak of the Cascade Range, Mount Rainier reigns as the centerpiece of the 365-square-mile park. It is a two-hour drive from Seattle-Tacoma, and draws more than a million visitors a year to Paradise Valley, the most popular portion of the park. All of them want to see the mountain when it is "out."

"There are people who think Rainier is a myth because it doesn't show every day, but it's not a hussy that's gonna just show it all, every day," said Ruth Kirk, who has studied and written extensively about Rainier. "It's just being quiet behind the cloak of gray sky."

Whether on a clear day or one wrapped in mist, early summer visitors can see avalanche lilies poke through snow with anemone, phlox, arnica and Indian paintbrush following to blanket the landscape. Each month brings a new palette of color to the park. Douglas-fir and hemlock forests endure, and gigantic Alaska yellow-cedars stand as they have for over a thousand years. It is not unusual to spot mountain goats, deer, elk, marmots, martens, grouse, thrushes, hawks, and ptarmigan, which share the park with their two-footed visitors.

With an average annual snowfall of 630 inches, what isn't snow and ice seems to be water. There are over 300 lakes—one seems to be cupped in every thawed crevasse—and 470 rivers and streams trickle or roar through the lush landscape. At one time visitors explored the blue maze of ice caves created by water flowing beneath the lower Paradise Glacier. The famous ice caves have disappeared, but

there's still plenty of ice on Rainier.

"Mount Rainier has more ice on it than all of the Cascade volcanoes combined," explained Park Superintendent Jon Jarvis, of the thirty-five square miles of snow and ice. The Nisqually Glacier, which extends from the summit on the south flank, is one of the most studied glaciers in the United States. "There is no place quite

Mount Rainier was designated a national park in 1899 to protect landscapes such as the glacial mountain and Reflection Lakes that capture its image, facing page, and wildlife including bobcats, above.

like that in the lower forty-eight where you can with a short walk or even a drive, be able to see glaciers like North America was covered with 10,000 years ago."

Nearly 10,000 climbers attempt to reach the summit of Mount Rainier annually (about half succeed), and, by the winter of 2001, sixty-eight climbers had lost their lives in the attempt. Most visitors stick to day hiking along the dozens of trails, but ninety-seven percent of the park is

designated as wilderness and the backcountry offers a total outdoors experience.

You can walk on a nature trail through the Trail of the Shadows, peer down into Box Canyon, or hike up to the face of a glacier. The ninety-three-mile trek along the Wonderland Trail is the ultimate backpacker's hike. If you find yourself here on a rainy day, consider the opinion of Ruth Kirk: "I think often we want the weather to be sunny and clear but, really, there's a lovely soft quality on a wet day, with the world kind of closed in upon itself."

In addition to its natural beauty, the park has been designated a National Historic Landmark District and one of the national park system's best examples of rustic park architecture and planning. Longmire Village is one of the park's oldest developed areas. You can take a walking tour of the district that includes the 1928 Administration Building, 1927 Community Building, 1910 Library, 1929 Gas Station, and 1911 General Store. Each illustrates the evolution of "parkitechture," as it came to be known. The National Park Inn, restored in 1989, has served as a hotel since 1926. A row of straight-back chairs still lines its front porch, where you can catch of glimpse of "the mountain" if it is out.

Mount Rainier, in 1928, was the first national park to implement a long-range plan. After its first centennial, it continues to evolve as a wonder-filled, compact park with its rain forests, alpine meadows, glaciers, historic architecture, and signature mountain.

The jagged volcanic peak of Mount Hood rises behind Timberline Lodge, above. Forest service architects and consultant Gilbert Stanley Underwood came together with a lodge design, facing page.

TIMBERLINE LODGE

OPENED 1938

Six miles up a winding road on Mount Hood, at the point where trees give way to volcanic ash, stands the 74,000-square-foot Timberline Lodge. This elegant piece of soft-gray architecture looks rather unimposing in contrast to the looming presence of Oregon's highest peak.

Looks can be deceiving: Timberline Lodge is more than a great lodge on a massive mountain.

Recognized as the first Works Progress Administration (WPA) project of its kind, it stands as a symbol of recovery. While the Great Depression was taking its toll on much of the nation, here on the slopes of Mount Hood, the New Deal administration of Franklin D. Roosevelt would create an example of what Americans could achieve under otherwise dire circumstances.

"It was crisis in this country, unparalleled, other than the Civil War," said forest service archeologist and historic preservation specialist Jeff Jaqua. "Franklin Roosevelt was elected to office because he promised to bring the country out of that. The hotel is a product of its time; you had recreation growing, you had skiing industry that was clamoring for a hotel on the mountain; you had the Great Depression. And then, FDR's response to that in the New Deal."

Timberline Lodge would be a WPA experiment, a plan to build and furnish the first recreational facility on public land with predominantly public funds. They would put hundreds of unemployed men and women to work and at the same time advance tourism in the state. Not only would the project embody public ownership of a recreational facility, but the building also would demonstrate that hand-crafted work linked to a region's heritage had its place in modern society.

For Timberline Lodge, that heritage began with native peoples of the western and eastern slopes of the Cascade Range—including Molalas, Kalapuya, Clackamas, Wascos and Sahaptin-speaking Warm Springs Indians—who hunted and gathered berries and food in the area.

It also included explorers Lewis and Clark, who first saw the mountain in 1805, Oregon Trail pioneers who cut the Barlow Trail on the south side of Mount Hood in 1845, and periodic volcanic eruptions that got everyone's attention.

Who could ignore an 11,235-foot high peak, complete with steaming fumaroles, spread over a base of ninety-two miles? A "sleeping" volcano with a razor sharp profile and moods to match?

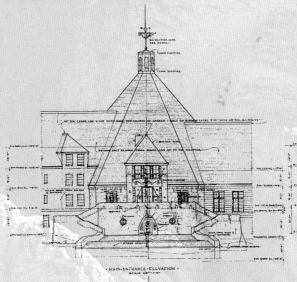

· MAIN·ENTRANCE·ELEVATION ·
SCALE 1/8"=1'0"

The mountain's mystery drew early adventurers to explore Mount Hood. The first recorded ascent was in 1845, and by the 1880s the mountain attracted recreational climbers.

In 1889, a small lodge—Cloud Cap Inn designed by Portland architects W.A. Whidden and Ion Lewis—was built on the northern slope of what was then the Cascade Range Forest Reserve. In 1908, the reserve was divided into several national forests including Oregon National Forest with Mount Hood as its center. The name was changed to Mount Hood National Forest in 1924, and a year later, the Mount Hood Loop Highway opened.

The mountain, once a playground for the elite, became a refuge from urban life for anyone with an automobile and a sense of adventure. Besides avid mountaineers, skiers also were making treks to the slopes, and the question of recreational development was hotly debated.

Emerson J. Griffith had long advocated a lodge on Mount Hood. Lack of funding or a cohesive management plan handicapped progress. Ironically, the Great Depression became the catalyst for development. Griffith was named WPA Director for Oregon. Griffith, with the support of Harry L. Hopkins, the WPA's first national administrator, threw himself into the project. Griffith quickly submitted an application to fund a recreation project, and on December 17, 1935, the WPA approved it.

The U.S. Forest Service granted land use for the construction of the lodge, planned for the southern slope of Mount Hood National Forest, an officially designated public recreation area.

STATELY HAND-CRAFTED WPA LEGACY
MOUNT HOOD NATIONAL FOREST, OREGON

Newel posts carved from telephone poles, left, and the glass tile murals of the Blue Ox Bar, below, are some of the details that make Timberline Lodge so special. Yet it is the grand scale of the "head house" that is the heart of the lodge, facing page.

With $20,000 seed money raised by the Mount Hood Development Association, a private organization formed in 1920 by a group of Portland businessmen who planned on managing the facility, and funds secured by Congress, a design had to be agreed upon.

The idea of a lodge on Mount Hood was not new, and a trail of rejected lodge plans proposed earlier for the northern slope paved the way for what would be a difficult process on the other side of the mountain. Frederick Law Olmsted, Jr., hired as a consultant by the U.S. Forest Service (USFS) and an original member of the Commission of Fine Arts, strongly objected to any modern "boxy-blocky" hotel plans.

Griffith wanted John Yeon, a young architect from a well-established Portland family, who had already made one rejected attempt on a Mount Hood hotel plan. This time, the Mount Hood Development Company, the forest service, and the head of Oregon's American Institute of Architecture all rejected Yeon's new low-slung concrete vision. Forest service officials in Washington, D.C., were getting impatient. They needed a well-respected "name" architect who was familiar with wilderness construction and design. They turned to a proven commodity.

Gilbert Stanley Underwood, who was working as Consulting Architect for the U.S. Treasury Department in Washington, D.C., and had left his mark at Yosemite, Bryce Canyon, Zion, and Grand Canyon national parks, was recommended for the job. Underwood's success had been his interpretation of rustic architect, using prodigious amounts of local stone and timber in hotel scale.

Underwood hoped that he, through his private company in Los Angeles, would be commissioned to design the lodge. He was "officially" named consulting architect. While Underwood worked in Washington, Stanley S. Stonaker represented Underwood & Company in Los Angeles; it was Stonaker, not Underwood, who made initial arrangements and took part in planning meetings.

Yet, it would not be Mr. Underwood who would spearhead the plan. This was, after all, a forest service project, and a group of architects working out of the USFS Portland office were anxious to show off regional themes and their own abilities.

While Underwood was working on the perspectives for a rustic lodge "of rough stones and timber, a sort of structure that will blend with the landscape rather than oppose it," apparently unknown to him, the forest service architects, with Tim Turner in charge, were drawing up their own plans. Turner coordinated the project, Linn Forrest—the youngest and only university trained architect of the group—drew the elevations, Howard Gifford created drawings for the interior, and Dean Wright rounded out the team.

In December 1935, the forest service architects submitted four preliminary schemes; most consisted of a three-part design made of stone and timber with ridge and gable roofs in the stately picturesque style of a country estate. In 1936, Underwood submitted his perspective drawings. His plan also called for three parts: an octagonal center lobby with a pointed "wigwam" roof oriented to the north, and two wings. The center of the octagon would have a "great circular fireplace…high, massive columns…with heavy log rail shelters all of peeled log construction held together with heavy hand-wrought iron bands," according to descriptions Stonaker submitted to the forest service.

Griffith, with both plans in hand, forwarded Turner's plans on to Underwood. Underwood, although naturally favoring his more rustic and

Works Progress Administration workers included women who wove, appliquéd, and sewed the lodge's accessories, top, and iron workers who forged the fabulous pieces that still fill the lodge, above.

rugged design, graciously acknowledged the work of the forest service team. Week by week, the forest service architects took over the project.

Underwood's original concept of a core lobby with a steeply pitched "wigwam" roof was changed from an octagon to a hexagon and turned to the south, following forest service recommendations. Instead of the "brutal" proportions Underwood desired, the lodge took on a more elegant, "picturesque" design.

What evolved was a style most often called "Cascadian" after the range of mountains Mount Hood is part of. The more refined, alpine design reflected not only Turner's, Forrest's and, in lesser part, Underwood's tastes, but also the times and location.

Instead of the rugged massive designs with the huge exterior logs of early great lodges, the shingled, board-and-batten, clapboard and stone exterior of Timberline paid homage to Portland just sixty miles away. Perhaps Underwood never fully understood that, unlike Yosemite Valley, Bryce Canyon and the Grand Canyon, Mount Hood was a familiar sight to most who went there. Instead of offering the wilds of the relatively unknown West or Southwest to rail passengers, as was the case at many national parks, Timberline Lodge was built for automobile travelers, mostly heading from the city for a quick mountain adventure. Turner and Forrest, both knowledgeable and comfortable with the Northwest vernacular, drew from the classic country estates found in and around Portland.

Still, the lodge holds true to the tenets of National Park Service rustic architecture and Olmsted's premise that the building must blend with the landscape. As Jeff Jaqua observed, "One of the design schemes for the building, and one of the parameters, was to use local materials. They wanted to showcase local

materials in the construction, as well as local artisans and craftsmen and architects on the lodge, in building the lodge. The lodge itself—it grows right out of the mountain, the way it's been designed and sited on the mountain."

While the architects hashed out the plans early in 1936, that exact site was still being sought. In May, resident engineer Ward Gano and landscape architect Emmett Blanchfield were dispatched to make a new topographic survey. Finally, on June 13, 1936, construction began. Located at the foot of Palmer snowfield at the 6,000-foot elevation, the site offered a view of the Cascade Range, including Mount Jefferson, Three-Fingered Jack and Mount Washington to the south, and the Mount Hood summit out the back door. It was also situated to accommodate a ski area—the potential draw to make Timberline Lodge a financially successful venture.

Logistics and administration of the project were difficult, with federal, state and local officials trying to wrangle control. A few crews set up camps in the winter; eventually almost 600 people worked on the project, with a goal of nine WPA workers for every one non-WPA worker.

The three-story west wing went up, then the two-story east wing. The hexagonal "head house" was built between the wingspans. After the foundation was poured, locally-quarried rubble masonry and uncut boulders were laid. The masons, many of them skilled Italian immigrants, worked into December laying the huge boulders and creating other stonework. Timberline's steeply pitched roof is covered with cedar shingles and broken by a number of hipped and shed-roofed dormer windows. The roof of the "head house" protrudes above the other rooflines much as the summit of Mount Hood stands above the landscape. A 750-pound

Masons hoist the stones into place.

through an arched stone tunnel and pine door embellished with a sculpted Indian. Soon after the lodge was built, an extension of the tunnel was added each winter to keep snowdrifts from blocking the entry. Stone staircases curve up from the ground-floor level to the first-floor entrance.

Inside, the ninety-two-foot-high hexagonal chimney rises from the lower-level lobby to the main lounge then through the ceiling. The chimney is actually six chimneys for six fire-places: three in the lower lounge and three in the main one. While builders set the six pine timbers in symmetrical spokes around the hub of the chimney, and set six forty-foot pines into the six angles of the "head house," a design concept was unfolding.

Griffith, with recommendations from the

bronze weather vane tops the chimney on the "head house" roof.

As classic as the exterior seems, hand-carved rams' heads topping the fir columns framing the first-level entry and a thunderbird carved on the lintel above it are indications of what is inside. Walk through the massive, 1,800-pound, hand-hewn ponderosa-pine door and the notions of architecture and art immediately come together.

Underwood wanted a far more rustic look with peeled logs, stone piers and crudely carved decorative details using Indian motifs—details he thought could be achieved economically by using WPA workers. Turner, with Howard Gifford doing most of the interior drawings, favored a more refined, finished look. The forest service won out. The "Timberline arch," a two-post and curved lintel design repeated through-out, came from Turner and Forrest. To Underwood, that sophistication represented "a little too much architecture" in the interior design. To the million tourists who come to the lodge each year, it is an architectural backdrop for the handcrafted details that are Timberline Lodge.

Underwood's two-entry concept of the "head house" was meant to separate hotel and recre-ational use. Skiers used the ground-level entry

On September 28, 1937, President Franklin D. Roosevelt dedicated Timberline Lodge.

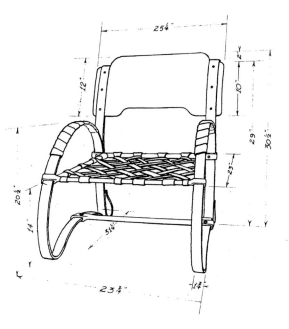

The "Timberline arch" sets off the Barlow Room entrance that frames the massive hand-carved doors. The iron, wood, and rawhide chairs were designed by Margery Hoffman Smith.

architects, had decided that blacksmithing, woodcarving and weaving would complement the architecture. To achieve this, Griffith hired O.B. Dawson to supervise the blacksmith work and Ray Neufer to oversee the wooden appointments. But it was Margery Hoffman Smith, an interior decorator from Portland, who pulled the style of Timberline Lodge together.

Smith was brought aboard when forest service administrators decided the project needed a "woman's touch." She wrote, "What an opportunity to use the work of fine artists to embellish the rooms!"

Griffith and Smith convinced WPA's Hopkins that the beautifully constructed lodge needed furnishings to match. An initial $39,000 was allocated. Nearly two years later, $100,000 had been spent. Eventually, the Fine Arts Division of the WPA provided money for the project. Even before funds had been found, Griffith had the architects adding detailed woodcarving and ironwork to their plans. In March 1936, using the wildlife and Indian and pioneer heritage of the region as her themes, Smith went to work.

The hand-forged wrought iron throughout Timberline is exquisite, from the coyote heads in

The ram's-head buffet table drawing was executed by wood workers, many trained as part of the WPA "experiment."

the Cascade Dining Room gate to hinges, escutcheons and doorknockers on the main door. Furniture fittings, window grilles, andirons (including some shaped like woodchucks, rabbits, and beavers), interior gates, light fixtures, chandeliers, and fittings for the ceiling beams were created in Dawson's Portland blacksmith shop using hand-held tools at the forge and anvil. Forest service architects originally proposed lantern chandeliers, but Underwood wanted wrought iron, and Smith concurred—one of his few contributions to the interior. Underwood

would not see the lodge until October 25, 1936. According to U.S. Forest Service "Notes on the Progress of Timberline Lodge," "Mr. Underwood expressed himself as generally pleased with the results to date and as far as could be ascertained, had little criticism to offer."

While the blacksmiths toiled, Ray Neufer's crew was busy doing woodwork for the lodge in the basement of a Portland high school. The lodge and furniture are of solid wood. The walls, beams, stairs, and railings are made from fir, while the floors are Oregon white oak. Other

Oregon woods—red cedar, Port Orford cedar, Western juniper and hemlock—were also used. The six huge "head house" timber supports (ponderosa pine harvested in Washington state) were all hand-hewn with broadax and adz. Newel post carvings of animals and birds were drawn by Portland artist Florence Thomas, then workers turned utility poles into what are some of the lodge's most beloved pieces. The wood carvers followed Gifford's detail designs, Indian motifs (some taken from a Camp Fire Girls handbook) for the thunderbird carving over the

The Cascade Dining Room is furnished with the original tables and chairs. Each chair features a variation of the "Timberline arch," above. Works Progress Administration workers forged the wrought-iron gates with coyote heads under the direction of O. B. Dawson, facing page.

main entrance and the Indian head on the ski lobby door.

Smith, with the help of Dawson and Neufer, designed almost every piece of furniture. Time was crucial, and workers were dispatched to create pieces before blueprints were drawn. If a design worked, the plan was drawn and additional pieces crafted.

The furniture reflects the bulk and size of the lodge—there is nothing delicate about the rawhide, wood, and iron furnishings. But there is subtlety. Every curve and arch of a doorway or window frame is repeated, whether on the back of a chair or on a chandelier. Smith later noted in a memo that she was not happy with the curved-back design of the dining room

chairs, but decided to repeat it "…and from the repetition gain a rhythm and pattern the single design does not possess."

That rhythm and pattern weave together as naturally as the hand-loomed fabrics Smith ordered. Weavers were recruited from the "white-collar projects" of Oregon's WPA. Eventually, about twenty women learned to work the looms and created nearly 1,000 yards of fabric for upholstery, drapes, and bedspreads. Smith selected twenty-three different motifs such as Bachelor Button, Zigzag, Cornflower, or Shooting Star for the forty-eight guestrooms. Appliqués made use of both an artistic vision and scraps of otherwise useless fabric left over from clothing relief programs. Rugs were hooked from discarded Civilian Conservation Corps uniforms and blankets.

As practical as some craft projects were, the artwork was not only aesthetic but also reflected both the region and the creation of the lodge. "The Spring on the Mountain" mosaic, designed by Thomas Laman; oil paintings by C.S. Price, one of Oregon's most distinguished artists; two large panels depicting the builders of Timberline, painted by Howard Sewall; and dozens of lithographs and watercolors all add to the living museum Timberline was to become. Douglas Lynch created a touch of whimsy with his incised linoleum murals in the ski grill (now the multimedia Barlow Room). Each panel, now carefully restored, illustrates one of Mount Hood's seasons in the "Calendar of Mountain Sports."

Apparently, Smith realized there was no bar in the lodge design. A wood-storage space was converted, and Portland artist Virginia Darcé designed the three panels and sign. The vivid fragments of opaque glass pieced into murals show the legendary Paul Bunyan and his blue ox, Babe, holding court in the tiny hideaway.

By August 1937, President Roosevelt indicated that he would be willing to dedicate the lodge during his trip to do the same for Bonneville Dam. A frenzy of work ensued, and the wrought-iron gate to the dining room, a special chair with arms for the president, and a handful of guestrooms were completed. On September 28, 1937, Roosevelt dedicated

Timberline Lodge in an address presented live over the radio.

The presidential event drained funds, and Turner in his log of October 14, 1937, was dismayed: "Due to the spending spree indulged in prior to the President's visit, there remains but some $6,000 for the completion of funds available. It is understood that $53,000.00 was expended within a three-week period immediately before the dedication."

The lodge didn't officially open until February 1938 and, when completed, it offered three levels of lodging, from perfectly-appointed "fireplace rooms" to dormitories.

The lodge's construction was both a WPA success and a failure. What originally had a price tag of less than a quarter-million dollars turned into a million-dollar undertaking. But the project did more than employ craftsmen and artists; there was also a teaching component in the project that expanded labor force while putting people to work. Emerson Griffith praised the WPA workers in a telegram:

"These men indeed feel that they are putting their skill into a cathedral. Coming up from the depths of despair they work with a spiritual exaltation which sometimes amazes me."

Still, it was argued that, for the amount of money spent, not enough workers were employed and Timberline's purpose as a recreation destination was not in keeping with WPA principles. Others took a longer view of the completed lodge, already considered an architectural masterpiece.

What is remarkable about Timberline Lodge is that so much of what was right, good, and pure about the project still lives. But it wasn't always so. The U.S. Forest Service, responsible for operating the facility, could not give the promised lease to the Mount Hood Development Company due to fears of conflict of interest. During the 1940s, Timberline Lodge, Inc., whose members included men who had been part of the original vision, operated the lodge. The building was closed during World War II, but postwar skiers brought new popularity to the mountain. When the company decided to get out of the lodge operation business, so began the structure's decline. The lodge was ignored and mismanaged until it was almost too late. Just two decades after it was built, Timberline Lodge was closed for nonpayment of utility bills.

Enter Richard Kohnstamm, a twenty-nine-year-old Easterner with a master's degree in social work and a love of skiing. Instead of hotel management experience, he had youth, optimism and family funds to get him going. Kohnstamm won the contract over 150 other applicants and reopened Timberline Lodge in December 1955. The first few years were financially challenging, but Kohnstamm upgraded skiing facilities, and the ski boom of the 1960s gave the new manager a much-needed boost. As business picked up and crowds flooded the lodge, the handcrafted furniture,

Today, volunteers continue to appliqué bedspreads, hook rugs, and make curtains for the lodge interior.

upholstery and drapes continued to take a beating. Kohnstamm concentrated on day-to-day operation of the complex's lodge, restaurant, bars, and gift shop—and skiing, maintenance and structural problems—until one day about a decade later when some guests with a sense of history arrived.

Rachael Griffin, former curator of the Portland Art Museum, "gave us a lecture," recalled Kohnstamm. "She said, 'You don't know what you have there. You have something of world importance.' So we sat with our heads down and tails between our legs." When Griffin was finished, Kohnstamm understood that the building he fell in love with was worth saving, and so were its furnishings. Two things were obvious: Timberline Lodge could no longer accommodate the growing crowds, and additional money would be needed to expand.

Kohnstamm helped lobby, with the forest service's endorsement, for congressional funding that resulted in the 1972 construction of the 19,500-foot conference center. Two large C.S. Price murals were moved from the Portland Art Museum and Portland Auditorium to the new addition that now bears the artist's name. By the time the conference center opened, hopes were high that a day lodge would be next. In 1980-1981, Wy'East Day Lodge was built. Timberline's ski lounge was remodeled, the front desk moved to ground level, and the Rachael Griffin Historic Exhibition Center created in 1986.

What gave restoration efforts a jump-start was the formation of Friends of Timberline. In 1975, Kohnstamm and Portland businessman John Mills founded the group and organized a twenty-nine-member board. With the lodge's proximity to Portland, people with power, talent, and knowledge joined in. Their mission was to preserve and document the artifacts, furnishings, structure, historical significance, and immediate environs of the lodge and to raise funds and volunteers to accomplish their goals. And so it began.

"Here you've got one of the biggest agencies in the country, a relatively small private company, and a tiny non-profit do-good, all contributing to do a part of a job that nobody could afford to do before," said John Mills of the cooperative effort.

In the fall of 1975, ten CETA (Comprehensive Employment Training Act) employees began work on hand-hooking rugs, and appliquéing and weaving fabric. All of the draperies in the main lobby and Cascade Dining Room, all of the upholstery fabric on every chair and sofa is hand-woven. Because this is a "living museum" full of guests and tourists, coverings and rugs must be replaced every five years.

As the curator of Timberline Lodge and one of the 1970s weavers and textile designers, Linny Adamson oversees the contemporary master craftsmen's work, researches the WPA color, line and design, and co-ordinates the overall visual style for the lodge. With a hands-on approach, she also trains volunteers. Finding the balance of the "then and now," aware of the need for preservation, and recreating the look, feel, and warmth is a never-ending job: "I look at this place like a big doll house; that's the only way I've been able to do it."

Fiber work is only the beginning: In one ten-year period, one hundred new wool rugs were hand-hooked, and the originals mended and put on display. Twice now, the seventy-three guestrooms' hand appliquéd draperies and handmade bedspreads have been re-done. Over 5,000 yards of fabric have been hand-woven. Restoration of priceless pieces of artwork and acquisitions are all part of the mandate. Conser-

Mount Hood is part of the Cascade Range; Timberline Lodge stands silhouetted against the other peaks including Mount Jefferson.

vators have restored numerous 1930s oil paintings and watercolors, replicas of wooden furniture have been built to meet hotel demands, and original pieces refinished due to heavy usage. Rawhide-laced chairs and lampshades have been re-created, often by volunteers. Iron gates, handrails, curtain rods and rings, and door latches have all been hand-forged.

"When you look at other hotels or other landmarks like Crater Lake, The Ahwahnee or Paradise Inn, they're wonderful places, but what's unique to us is that the craftsmen never really stopped creating for the building. In this day and age, especially now that we're in the next century, into the millennium, we're still believing that the craftsmen have a place," Linny Adamson said.

One of those craftsmen is Darryl Nelson, who has carried on O.B. Dawson's ironwork. Nelson is a third-generation Timberline black-

smith who followed in the footsteps of Russell Maugins, a commercial pilot and blacksmith volunteer. It was Maugins who tracked down O.B. Dawson, then retired in Florida, and brought Dawson back to Timberline. Here the master blacksmith explained his work. Maugins listened, learned, then took on the restoration and replacement of the ironwork. Maugins then met Nelson through the Northwest Blacksmiths Association, and they joined forces on Timberline projects. When Maugins passed away, Nelson carried on.

As Nelson put it: "The best compliment they can give us is when we see someone looking at iron we just put in and they're saying, 'Boy, they don't make stuff like this anymore'."

Timberline Lodge is a "Depression-era baby," and its management has evolved as a partnership among the government, nonprofit groups, and for-profit interests. RLK Company

(now managed by Richard Kohnstamm's son, Jeff), the U.S. Forest Service, and Friends of Timberline are a triumvirate whose abiding respect for history makes the continuing saga of Timberline Lodge possible.

"With Timberline, you think of what President Roosevelt said: He dedicated the lodge to the 'faithful skill and performance of the people, for generations to come.' And I loved his words and I still believe it," Linny Adamson explained as she surveyed her "doll house."

Timberline Lodge is a product of its time. A time when Americans had discovered the joy and luxury of recreation, when the skiing industry longed for a hotel on the mountain, and when what should have dampened all of that enthusiasm—the Great Depression—instead ignited the creativity and imagination of hundreds of men and women.

Mount Hood rises as Oregon's highest peak and is reflected in Trillium Lake, above. Rhododendrons bloom in profusion in the national forest, facing page.

MOUNT HOOD NATIONAL FOREST

THE DRAW OF THE PEAK

Responding to the June 12, 1894. advertisement run in Portland's *Morning Oregonian:* "To Mountain Climbers and Lovers of Nature...It has been decided to meet on the summit of Mount Hood on the 19th of next month...," more than 300 people encamped on the flanks of Mount Hood on July 18. By 8:00 a.m. the next day, the first climbing party of 107 reached the summit, followed by the rest of the 193 men and women. Of those, 105 climbers formed the mountaineering Mazamas Club as charter members.

The thrill of the climb makes Mount Hood one of the world's most climbed peaks, second only to Japan's Mount Fujiyama. Due, in part, to easy access from a metropolitan area, hikers often underestimate the power of the peak. About a dozen climbers are rescued each year. Anyone who asks about the "walk" to the summit is immediately set straight. This is a technical climb.

While climbers first ruled the mountain, with an average snow base of 175 to 200 inches each season and snowfall from 300 to 400 inches per year, Mount Hood became a mecca for skiers. Timberline Ski Area offers skiing and boarding year round, except for a few weeks in October when it is closed down for maintenance and repair. The mountain also hosts Mount Hood Meadows, Cooper Spur, Multorpor/Ski Bowl and Summit ski areas.

Timberline Lodge is the only "great lodge" in a national forest, but one mile above the lumbering lodge is a miniature version of the Cascadian masterpiece. In 1939, the Works Progress Administration constructed Silcox Hut, built as the terminus for the original Magic Mile chairlift. The L-shaped "hut" embraces the same workmanship of its parent building. Restored and reopened in 1993, it is another example of rustic mountain architecture and is on the National Register of Historic Places. It's an unforgettable experience to walk to the hut, watch the sun fall behind the Cascade Range and the sky fill with stars, be served a fabulous meal, then bunk down for the night in this intimate setting. The hut is rented to groups or, in May, individuals can make reservations for the night.

You need not be a climber or skier to revel in the majesty of Mount Hood National Forest. The easiest and most panoramic way to see the mountain is from Timberline's Magic Mile Super Express chairlift that takes sightseers to the 7,000-foot level.

And then there are the hiking trails. Over 1,170 miles of trails wind through the forest that stretches from Columbia River National Scenic Area to the Mount Jefferson Wilderness. The visual center of the 1.1-million-acre national forest is Mount Hood, part of the Cascade Range that runs from Mount Lassen in Northern California to Mount Garibaldi in British Columbia. Of that, 186,213 acres are designated wilderness areas. The largest is the Mount Hood Wilderness, which includes the mountain's cragged peak and upper slopes. Lakes, streams, waterfalls, alpine meadows, and dense forest cover the mountainous area where camping, hiking, fishing, mountain biking, and snow shoeing are favored pastimes.

The forest graces both the western and eastern sides of the Cascade Range, so the high elevations of rock, sand and pumice give way to timbered slopes, with mountain hemlock most abundant on the wet west side and subalpine fir on the more arid eastern slope. Grand Douglas-fir dominates the lower western slopes amid noble and silver firs and whitebark pines. Growing beneath the canopy of evergreens are huckleberry, vinemaple, and Oregon grape, with lush stands of rhododendron.

This panorama is habitat to nearly 150 species of birds from tiny hummingbirds to bald eagles and the northern spotted owl. Shrews, bats, marmots, bears, mountain lions, deer, and elk are some of the forty mammal species that inhabit the mountain.

The mission of the national forests is quite different from that of the national parks. Mount Hood National Forest falls under the domain of the U.S. Department of Agriculture, while national parks are operated through the Department of the Interior. The forest service is an agency whose goal is to manage lands owned by the American public. That management covers a wide range of uses including clean water, recreation opportunities, and timber production.

In the 1920s and '30s the U.S. Forest Service was presented an opportunity to make management decisions for a type of landscape that normally fell to the National Park Service. At the time, timber production was not as important as it would become for the forest service after World War II. A preservation land ethic was strong within the agency, and forest service managers and planners of the era were anxious to show they understood the mountain's inherent values.

Timberline Lodge and the recreation opportunities found at Mount Hood were part of a grand scheme devised during a dark time in U.S. history. They remain intertwined with the challenge of meeting the demands of those interested in preservation, conservation, and resource management.

The cedar-bark-covered, ten-sided chateau seems to grow from the ravine, above. Local contractor Gust Lium selected the site and drew the plans for the chateau, facing page.

Tucked into the Siskiyou Mountains in the southwestern portion of Oregon is one of the state's best kept secrets. Oregon Caves is among America's earliest national monuments, set aside in 1909 to preserve the marble caverns that stretched deep into the mountainside.

As worthy of preservation is the bark-covered Oregon Caves Chateau that straddles the ravine across the plaza from the caves' opening. Part of a small complex of buildings that began taking shape in the 1920s, it stands as one of the last examples of a hotel built on public lands in the rustic picturesque style of architecture. Besides having status as a prime example of organic architecture, it survives as a place from another time.

"The chateau is an integral part of the whole landscape," explained John Roth, National Park Service (NPS) natural resources specialist. "It's a refuge, if you will, a place to rest and recuperate and get away from it all."

Unlike many of the lodges in western national parks, it was not designed by an up-and-coming Los Angeles or Chicago architect. Gust Lium, an established local contractor from nearby Grants Pass, designed and built Oregon Caves Chateau. Familiar with the area and materials at hand, he designed it to fill the gorge and hug the embankments, and topped it with a steeply pitched gable roof broken by shed and gable dormers, creating a roofline as jagged as a mountain range. The six-story, ten-sided lodge, covered in shaggy cedar bark and shingled in wood shakes, seems to have been dropped into the ground as a seedling. It simply sprouts up two stories from the roadway, part of the natural landscape, the lower four floors forming a root-like structure.

National Park Service historian Steve Mark, who first worked at Oregon Caves in 1977, is one of the chateau's many admirers: "You have to say, when you look at Oregon Caves Chateau, that it's a brilliant piece of work. Just describing it: it's so irregular. All the sides are different; window shapes and sizes are very different, and yet, the thing works."

Fascination with the man-made architecture at Oregon Caves is only fitting, since interest in this woodsy niche of rugged land began with the discovery of one of Mother Nature's architectural wonders.

In 1874, Elijah Davidson discovered a cave entrance while hunting, and soon the cavern became the destination for groups of adventurers. With a ball of string to guide them out, they would crawl into the bowels of the earth carrying burning boughs and candles to light the way, then break off stalactites and stalagmites to prove they had indeed been where few had ventured.

Small outfitters and miners began taking out mineral claims around the cave and putting together expeditions to explore them. Trails were cut and a cabin constructed. Around 1887, the Oregon Caves Improvement Company was established, but financial setbacks, lack of title to the land, and difficult access to the site tabled any grand development. Still, a fascination with the caves prevailed, and the *San Francisco Examiner,* backed by owner William Randolph Hearst, sponsored a well-publicized expedition with the intent of promoting the caves' development.

In 1906, the Siskiyou National Forest was established, and mineral development around the caves was banned the following year. On July 12, 1909, the 480-acre site was set aside as the country's twentieth national monument. The proclamation read: "Any use of the land which interferes with its preservation or protection as a National Monument is hereby forbidden." That year 360 visitors came to the caves; one of them was the "Poet of the Sierra," Joaquin Miller, who then penned an article for *Sunset* magazine about "Oregon's wondrous marble halls."

Still, it wasn't until 1922, when a road reached the

A variety of Oregon wood was used to build the open stairway, above, that overlooks the pond created from the water of Cave Creek, facing page.

cave entrance area, that any organized development took place. The U.S. Forest Service (USFS) drafted plans for cottages, electrical lighting, and steel ladders inside the caves.

The following year, a group of Grants Pass businessmen secured a permit to provide guide services and build a resort. The Oregon Caves Resort (later named Oregon Caves Company) was made up of men with more than an eye on the dollar. They had a vision of what the development should be, and hired Arthur L. Peck to help develop the site plan. It was Peck, a faculty member of the Oregon Agricultural College, who envisioned a gable-roofed chalet near the cave entrance. And it was Peck who called for the Port Orford cedar-bark sheathing that would swathe all of the structures.

Like Crater Lake Lodge on the rim of Crater Lake and Old Faithful Inn at Old Faithful Geyser in Yellowstone, Oregon Caves Chateau is as much a part of the monument's image as the cave itself. While the chateau is now the centerpiece structure, the original chalet and a number of smaller buildings first defined the architectural style. The architect of the chalet (which was replaced in 1942) is unknown, but the building featured Peck's design and material specification. A nursery, "Kiddy Kave," was completed in 1924.

When the Redwood Highway connecting Grants Pass with Crescent City, California, opened in 1926, seven guest cottages were added to the village, each nestled amongst the trees. Gust Lium, who became synonymous with Oregon Caves architecture, designed the cottages. Lium was the brother-in-law of Sam Baker, one of the founders of the Oregon Caves Resort. Lium had an excellent reputation, and his private homes and commercial buildings reflected both his creative approaches to architecture and his building expertise.

When it was time to tackle the main building, Baker explained to Lium that the company wanted a fifty-room chateau with a large comfortable lobby with fireplace plus a dining area with connecting ballroom. The question was where to build it within the steeply pitched landscape.

Lium looked around, then down into the ravine of Cave Creek Canyon. That was where he would wedge the chateau. Baker accepted the location recommendation, but a design review by the forest service was required. Lium drew perspective views of the chateau that do not show exact elevations, but clearly indicate the variations of the three rectangular shapes that resulted in the ten-sided hotel. The two rectangular wings bank the sides of the canyon, with the conical center expanding as the building rises from the ravine.

Construction began in September 1931, delayed by the start of the Great Depression, and the chateau opened in May 1934. Lium and a small crew of men created the building on a reinforced concrete foundation with post and beam interior supports. Most of the lumber was harvested from the Grayback drainage, about eight miles from the monument. The cedar-bark sheathing came from a railroad-tie cutting operation in the same area, and redwood was purchased from a regional supplier in California. Interior finishing woods, including ponderosa pine, madrone, white oak, and Douglas-fir, were cut locally. Native limestone and marble were quarried for the fireplace. The materials meshed perfectly, and Lium constructed the chateau for $50,000.

The first floor, deep in the ravine, houses the furnace, sprinkler system, and machine shop. Storage and the employee dining room fill the second floor. The design flares as it goes up; the much-larger third floor includes the dining

A conduit routes water through the center of the dining room.

space, visitors must first adjust to the low light, then take a long horizontal view of the room. Even with huge picture windows, the lobby has an aura as deep as the densely forested gully it straddles, as mysterious as the limestone-and-marble caves that were the reason for the lodge's very existence.

One must sit in front of the massive limestone and marble double-sided fireplace as the flames pop and flicker to fully appreciate the chateau. This is John Roth's favorite place in the chateau. "That huge marble fireplace really illustrates that refuge aspect of the chateau; it's a comforting part of the building," he explained as he relaxed before the hearth. "I think that humans have a potentially fatal flaw, and that is to be obsessed with ourselves too much; and both the beauty—the natural beauty of the cave, and the beauty of the chateau—helps us get away from ourselves."

Eyes adjust to the darkness of wood lighted only by firelight and the chandeliers, whose now-fragile parchment shades cast an amber glow to the huge lobby as someone picks a tune on the Welder baby grand piano. Thirty-inch-thick peeled log posts, harvested from the nearby mountains, hold the massive beams. Details in the workmanship include the blind joints, lapped and dovetailed, along with decorative accents like the wooden plugs and dowels. Redwood wainscoting covers the lower portion of the walls and "Nu-Wood" pressed-fiberboard panels blanket the top. Fred Kiser hand-colored photographs dominate the walls.

The open stairwell showcases a profusion of Oregon woods, featuring split oak steps resting on notched log stringers, lodgepole pine newel posts, and peeled madrone balustrades polished to a rich mahogany glow, topped with fir hand-rails. A two-story window with a view of the pond and falls serves as the stairway's backdrop.

room, ballroom, coffee shop, and kitchen. Windows bank each end of the dining room where one of the chateau's most unique features flows. Outside, a waterfall and a pond catch Cave Creek, then a conduit routes the stream through the dining room. Designed before Frank Lloyd Wright's acclaimed Fallingwater House at Bear Run, Pennsylvania, it illustrates Lium's

understanding of the relationship between nature and architecture.

Yet the full impact of Lium's genius unfolds in the fourth-floor lobby, accessed from the main entrance off the parking plaza. Unlike those of most of the lodges in this book, the chateau's lobby is a single story. Instead of their eyes immediately going up to a huge soaring

The great hall with its low ceiling and dim lighting reflects the atmosphere of the monument's cave and forest, lower right. Monterey furniture, including the two chairs by the limestone fireplace, far right, and the writing desk, remain from when the chateau opened.

A bit of serendipity seems to have transpired in the selection of furniture. Originally ordered from a Portland department store, the Monterey furniture that fills the hotel is now the largest extant collection of what has become a highly valued style. In 1929, Mason Manufacturing Company in Los Angeles, originally known for its iron work and iron lamps, had begun designing and hand crafting the 120-piece Monterey line.

The wooden sofas, chairs, desks, secretaries, dining room and bedroom sets, and wrought iron accessories, had the aura of Western movie sets of the era. It's no wonder, according to eighty-nine-year-old George Mason (the man responsible for designing the line, and son of co-owner Frank Mason): the first settee replicated a piece in a Warner Brothers movie. Monterey furniture soon filled the Spanish revival and ranch homes spreading across southern California, and celebrities' estates including those of Will Rogers, Walt Disney, Roy Rogers, and Gene Autry.

Each piece was quality built, handmade of Oregon alder, carved, bruised, buffed then finished. The wood furniture with hand-forged wrought iron hinges and straps, rope seat supports, and hand-painted wildflower and desert scenes was selected for its rustic charm and created yet another unusual feature in the chateau.

The wood is oil- or base-stained then coated with a wax polish. The company also devised a bleached wood, desert dust finish. Examples of both can be found at the chateau. Many of the pieces, particularly in the guestrooms, feature hand-painted wild flowers and desert scenes. The company trademark, a horseshoe branded into the wood, marks the earliest pieces.

The chalet entrance framed a view of the chateau, below. In December 1964 a torrent of melting snow, rainwater, and forest debris rushed through the arched opening, nearly destroying Oregon Caves Chateau, left.

The Monterey line was manufactured until 1943, when the founder, Frank Mason, died. George was drafted, and his mother and his father's partner sold the factory.

The chateau's collection of Monterey was once much larger. In December 1964, the dining room furniture was lost in a catastrophic event that nearly destroyed the chateau.

Harry Christiansen had just taken over as lodge manager, and after a successful summer season, he was supervising the lodge for the winter with his wife, and assistant manager Bob Hines. In mid-December near-record snowfall was followed by a freak rainstorm.

"I was looking out the window of my apartment on the second floor of the hotel, and I noticed that there was a trickle of water coming through the archway of the chalet," Christiansen recalled on a visit to the chateau in the fall of 2000. "I suddenly said to Bob: 'What's that noise?' And he looked at me and his eyes popped open, and he said: 'I don't know what it is, but run!' He went scrambling up the stairway to his apartment and I ran down the driveway. All I can remember of that at the moment is a big log chasing me. I later made firewood out of that log; it was forty-eight inches in diameter."

The sudden winter flood had sent tons of water and debris down on the chateau. When the flood of rocks, logs, and silt stopped, the dining room—decorated for holiday guests— and two lower floors were filled with gravel and rock. Steps were ripped from the staircase, French doors torn from the hinges. The entire foundation had slipped. It looked as if the chateau was a total loss.

"I had a meeting with the Board of Directors that following week down in Grants Pass," explained Christiansen. "I said: 'I'm sorry, gentlemen, ladies—it's too bad, but the chateau is gone,

the dining room is ruined, coffee shop is a mess, the kitchen is full of mud, everything downstairs, it's completely covered. I wouldn't give you a nickel for the place!'"

The directors, however, did not agree. They insisted that Christiansen get the chateau in working order. Gust Lium was brought in to direct workers in gently moving the mammoth structure back into place. Lium, then in his late eighties, died months after the flood.

Most of the damage was in the lower three floors, but the original balustrades on the open stairway had to be replaced. The maple floor in the dining room was ruined and replaced with plywood subfloor and carpeting. African cherry paneling replaced the original wainscoting.

"And, believe it or not, we did it. On the twenty-sixth of May, we opened this hotel, back in the same condition, literally, that it was before the flood," said Christiansen with pride.

Part of that restoration was the coffee shop where visitors can still order old-fashioned malted milks and shakes. Original knotty pine paneling, birch and maple counters, and stainless steel stools with bright red vinyl seats, line the soda fountain area.

Guestrooms in the chateau are as varied as the roofline. The original furnishings are still in most of the rooms except on the first floor, where an unfortunate replacement of the Monterey pieces with motel-like Mediterranean furniture took place in the 1970s, but they will be replaced with Monterey reproductions. Every room has a view, and the attic rooms with their pitched ceilings offer special hideaways.

The National Park Service was into its "rustic" period when, under an Executive Order, it inherited administration of Camp Oregon Caves in 1933. What it found was a project in

Oregon Caves Chateau remains a prime example of organic rustic architecture.

keeping with NPS philosophy. Striving for "harmony" between man-made structures and the environment drove the rustic design philosophy of the time.

At approximately the same time that the NPS took over, the chateau opened and the Civilian Conservation Corps (CCC) set up camp at the confluence of Sucker and Grayback creeks eight miles west of the monument. CCC projects gave the park service the necessary funds and manpower to plan for and execute a series of roads, trails and landscape work. At that time, the best and the brightest in the field of landscape design worked for the government, and the stone walls, steps, and native flora plantings they designed have seasoned well.

Retaining walls forming the chalet courtyard and the fishpond below had been built in 1929. The two ponds created from water diverted from Cave Creek, and dry-laid stonework built with rough cut limestone and marble from the cave, are CCC projects. The road system, parking areas, and trail system, all environmentally compatible, were completed by 1935. The checking and comfort station, native rock walls, and peeled-log pole roadway lights are all pre-1940. The integrated use of cedar-bark sheath-

ing and native stone masonry set a precedent for state park and USFS architecture throughout the Siskiyou National Forest.

The "alpine village" of Arthur Peck's vision and Gust Lium's execution, complemented by the landscape design of the U.S. Forest Service and NPS, seems little changed since the era when this National Historic Monument took form.

The cabins and Kiddie Kave are gone, but Lium designed and built the three-story, asymmetrical chalet with its steeply pitched-roof breezeway, the gathering point for cave tours. A ranger's residence, designed by Crater Lake National Park's resident landscape architect, Francis Lange, was built in 1935-1936, nestled in the forest above the chalet. The guide dormitory, built in 1927, was expanded in 1940 and 1972, and features peaked dormers. Unlike in many parks, its additions are true to the original vision.

The U.S. government owns the building and it is managed by a private concessionaire under NPS direction.

Oregon Caves development is a lesson in "less is more." This small canyon, cut into the Siskiyou Mountains by Cave Creek, accessed by a twenty-mile-long, winding, two-lane road, is unlike the panoramic settings of other great lodges. It is an introspective experience to stay at Oregon Caves Chateau. Here, a cocoon-like setting pulls visitors into nature's fold, much like descending into the caverns.

"I love this place, and I'll always love it," said Harry Christiansen as his eyes gazed across the lobby. "It's a beautiful place and a wonderful thing, and thank God it's still here."

The heart of the monument is within the mountain, where formations like Millers Chapel are now protectd by airlocks that control airflow through the tunnels, above. Old-growth ponderosas are part of the forest that blankets the Siskiyou Mountains, facing page.

OREGON CAVES NATIONAL MONUMENT

A POCKET OF NATURAL DIVERSITY

The winding canyon road from Cave Junction to the monument offers a perfect introduction to this intimate enclave. A canopy of mixed broadleaf and conifer forests covers the steeply pitched terrain. Oregon maple, Pacific madrone, ponderosa and sugar pines, grand and white firs, Port Orford and incense cedars, along with Douglas-fir, fill the upper reaches with a blanket of vinemaple, chinkapin, laurel, madrone, and feathery ferns covering the ground.

Fog lingers in the winter and early spring, and sunshine streams through the treetops in the summer. Fifty inches of rainfall and 160 inches of snow keep the landscape lush.

The 480-acre monument may be small, but it is chock full of natural treasures. Situated seven miles north of the California/Oregon boundary and forty miles east of the Pacific Coast, the monument attracts about 90,000 tourists each year.

What you find is an intimate and friendly place where park rangers offer interpretive programs that are as much fun as they are informative. From mid-March to December, ninety-minute cave tours lead groups of no more than sixteen through those "wondrous marble halls." The only lodging is the chateau that usually closes for the winter; campgrounds are available in adjoining Siskiyou National Forest.

The main development is on a natural bench that arches in front of the cave entrance. Loop trails cut through the forests; the longest is only six miles. A short hike through old growth forest takes you to Big Tree, a Douglas-fir with the widest tree girth known in Oregon.

The setting of old growth forests and jutting peaks is the icing on the cake. The heart of the monument lies within the cave system. Park naturalists explain that the Siskiyou Mountains began as large chunks of ocean crust. The marble outcrops that formed the caves were once a limestone reef growing on top of an active volcano in a geologic setting known as a back-arc basin. The continent was pushed over the reef, burying it nearly twelve miles under the continent's edge. The reef then uplifted to 4,000 feet above sea level. This all took 194 million years.

Early spelunkers crawled through the cave entrance. During the 1930s, workers blasted passageways and expanded the entry. Human contact left more than debris and vandalism in its wake. The entire cave's ecosystem was altered as airflows changed, inappropriate walkways were built and lighting disrupted the fragile internal balance of the cave. One of the most extensive restoration projects of any American cave began in 1986. Fifteen hundred tons of rubble were removed, lighting reduced to control the algae, and a new trail laid.

Airlocks now control the airflow from the tunnels and some of the formations have been repaired.

What you find during the 0.6-mile tour is an adventure in geology and underworld life. The caverns remain in the 40°s F., and the damp dripping passages are rimmed with striking formations. The calcite stalactites and stalagmites share the stage with the petal-like flowstone at Paradise Lost and the rib formations of Passageway of the Whale, only a few of the eerie sights. Cave creatures are often secretive, but you may see daddy longlegs, crickets, moths, and bats.

One of the recent finds within the caves is a treasure trove of fossil bones from the Ice Age. Bear, jaguar, amphibians, and bats are some of the fifteen species whose remains are preserved within the cave—making it one of the most important cave fossil sites in the West.

A visit to Oregon Caves National Monument is a compact journey back in time. "We may be small," said John Roth, park resources specialist, "but we have some of the most concentrated diversity of rocks and life found on or in our planet."

The once decrepit Crater Lake Lodge was born again when the building was dismantled and rebuilt, above. Mark Daniels' 1914 vision of the great hall with stenciling and additional supports was never realized, facing page.

CRATER LAKE LODGE

OPENED 1915

Northeast of Oregon Caves, just beyond the point where the Siskiyou Mountains converge with the southern peaks of the Cascade Range, is Crater Lake. Cupped in half a million years of volcanic accumulation, the midnight blue lake is one of nature's most majestic surprises.

Native peoples had long known of the huge water-filled caldera, but a generation passed from the time the first white explorers tramped in the Cascade Range until a group of prospectors stumbled upon the lake. When John Wesley Hillman rode to the rim while searching for gold in 1853, he found a treasure that would be far more lasting. Laid out before his party of ragtag prospectors, he later recalled, was the bluest lake he had ever seen. With a depth of almost 2,000 feet and a skirt of pumice, it was one of the wonders of the world.

Over the next twenty years a wagon road allowed access to the lake's south side, and military and geologic expeditions—along with intrepid early tourists—documented visits to the "Great Sunken Lake."

But it was the 1885 trip of William G. Steel, who hiked with friends to the rim of Crater Lake, that changed its status. Simply put, Steel was overwhelmed by the scene. He returned often, and in 1896, as part of the Mazamas mountaineering club, he repeatedly came back to promote the lake and its surroundings as a candidate for a national park. In 1902, Crater Lake National Park was established, mostly through Steel's seventeen-year crusade, and with it came the real possibility of building a hotel.

The construction, deterioration, and resurrection of Crater Lake Lodge play an integral role in the park's history. Opened in 1915, the original lodge was finally closed in 1989, and the building visitors see today reopened in 1995 to stand as William Gladstone Steel's "dream" hotel finally become reality.

Steel's original dream began to take shape in 1907, when he formed the Crater Lake Company. As its president, one of his first projects was not a hotel, but a modest tent city where tourists spent the night. Visitors found primitive lodging, hot meals, and the chance to indulge in the spectacular surroundings. Steel longed for grander things—steamboats cruising to Wizard Island, elevators descending to the water's edge, and two hotels. But he knew he could not do it alone.

He longed for railway financing, the kind of money that made Old Faithful Inn in Yellowstone and El Tovar at the Grand Canyon signature hotels. Southern Pacific rail baron Edward Henry Harriman visited the site in 1908, but his sudden death a year later put an end to Steel's hope for a railway-financed hotel at the northeast side of the lake accessed by the rail line. "Of the two hotels planned, only one was built and that happened to be an automobile lodge," explained NPS historian Steve Mark.

That lack of funding would plague the project for decades to come. Yet Steel was not about to abandon his dream. Soon after Harriman's death, Steel named Portland developer and real estate associate Alfred L. Parkhurst as the company's general manager, major stockholder, and much-needed financier. Parkhurst set out to make Steel's dreams a reality. The agenda included developing the necessary utilities, and then building a lodge. Portland architect

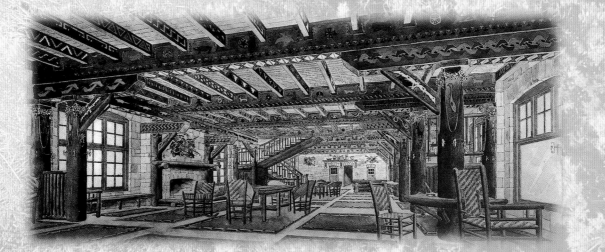

THE LODGE OREGONIANS WOULDN'T LET DIE

CRATER LAKE NATIONAL PARK, OREGON

*Early visitors
camped near the lake's rim.*

R.H. Hockenberry drew the plans, and contractor Frank Keyes took on the daunting task of constructing the lodge during the few months the area wasn't buried in snow.

In 1909, few lodges existed at high elevations with heavy snow conditions. Parkhurst and Hockenberry could have turned to Cloud Cap Inn on Mount Hood, also in the Cascade Range, or a smaller version of Robert Reamer's Old Faithful Inn at Yellowstone. Instead, Hockenberry followed Parkhurst's lead and his own experience, and designed a lodge that combined the idea of an "auto-lodge" with that of a suburban house, relying on mock Tudor design.

While later lodges like those in Glacier National Park, Mount Rainier National Park, and Mount Hood National Forest, were constructed of heavy timbers and logs, Crater Lake Lodge was basically a light wood-frame building much like homes of the period.

The incorporation of native rock for the first floor wall structure helped make it blend with the setting. Three rectangular sections hugged the edge of the caldera, with a kitchen wing joined on the south end at a ninety-degree angle. Eaves began just above the second story, with shed roof dormers for the third-story rooms, and a row of fourth-story dormers. Two stone chimneys for fireplaces in the dining hall and great hall, along with a third outdoor fireplace, added interest to the design.

Topped with a steeply pitched roof with jerkinhead rather than traditional gables and slightly varied roofline, the silhouette blends with its setting. The roof, according to a newspaper interview with Keyes, was to be tiling, and "...will defy the ravages of the elements for all time to come." Instead, probably because builders knew that the frame would not hold the weight of tile, it was shingled with wood and eventually stained a dark green.

Building the lodge was a task few at the time would consider—and one Parkhurst and Keyes underestimated. The project was never properly funded. From the original estimate of $5,000, the cost soon soared to $30,000. Keyes often ignored Hockenberry's plans, taking shortcuts to save money. The contractor struggled to get the necessary equipment and supplies. Timber, rocks, and stone were in abundant supply, but quarrying stone and moving timber to the site were fraught with mishaps. Getting supplies to the edge of Crater Lake was just a fraction of the battle.

In 1911, Parkhurst reported that lumber was at the construction site, but he couldn't secure carpenters to do the work. With only the summer months in which to build, Keyes competed for labor during the harvest season. After the lodge slowly took form each summer, winter would ravage the structure. One of the unfortunate shortcuts was to forgo strong roof trusses necessary to support the lodge from snow and wind. During the winter of 1913-1914, much of the roof collapsed—an omen of the structural difficulties that would plague the lodge.

While the lodge was under construction, Mark Daniels, the first general superintendent and landscape engineer for the national parks, consulted with Steel and Parkhurst, and a development plan for the park—Rim Village—took shape. Daniels not only outlined priorities for national park development, but as a private consultant, he drew up the plans for the lodge's great hall. Daniels' drawing shows an elaborate European great hall that offers a hint of what Crater Lake Lodge—the dream—was all about, but also shows additional interior supports that would have added to its structural stability. There weren't funds for such a luxurious design, and once again ignoring additional structural components, the great hall was simplified.

Instead of the great hall's more refined interior look, it was decided to use bark-covered logs on the interior walls and stairways for a rustic demeanor.

The scheduled 1912 opening passed, but the upcoming World's Fair in the San Francisco and the prospects of a flood of tourists up the coast prompted an acceleration in construction. A still unfinished Crater Lake Lodge opened the summer of 1915. Tarpaper, not wood, covered the planned battened-board exterior, and fiberboard separated the rooms. Bathrooms were usually shared, and a generator provided erratic power.

Yet the people came. If the rooms left much to be desired, the setting did not. Straddling a knife's edge between two environments—the great caldera on one side and the Klamath Basin to the south—it sat perched between two worlds.

Lodge construction began on the edge of the caldera in 1909, above, and by 1923, a much needed annex was being built, top.

The interior of the great hall was rustic with rubble stone fireplaces, and unpeeled logs on the walls, above. The transformation of the great hall included numbering the stones and rebuilding the fireplace, and selecting rustic and Arts and Crafts style furnishings, facing page.

Visitors could find a seat at one of the great hall windows and gaze over the deep blue waters of Crater Lake. The massive fireplaces offered warmth, and the haven was certainly a step up from the tents that were still available. With all of its problems, Crater Lake Lodge had become a destination. Its being an auto-lodge proved a success and, as automobile ownership exploded in the late 1910s and early 1920s,

visitation could double in a year.

As the crowds grew, so did the complaints. Parkhurst struggled with the situation. By 1919, National Park Service Director Stephen Mather was furious, viewing Crater Lake Lodge as a blemish on the National Park Service's growing list of lodges. He didn't let up. In 1921, Parkhurst forfeited his lease under pressure, and Crater Lake Lodge Company, under the direc-

tion of Eric V. Hauser and Richard W. Price, took over the daunting task of running the lodge, and the park service began promoting it.

Still the lodge was not finished. The new concessionaires pumped money into upgrades and additions starting in 1923. Fire escapes gripped the exterior, but structural problems and the bland interior remained much the same. Two annexes, in keeping with the stone, wood, and windows of the main lodge, were built. The project was completed in segments each summer, but twenty years later, rooms were still unfinished or unused.

"The lodge's problems stem from the reason for most business failure, under-capitalization," said Steve Mark. "Not enough money, a short construction season…Those conspired to produce a lodge that was dramatically under-built and took forever to be completed."

While the use of native materials—unpeeled logs, wood shingles, and stone—was consistent with the idea that park buildings should blend with the environment, the lodge, perched 1,000 feet above the rim, would always be an "eye-sore" to the purists whose influence on NPS building was growing. By 1943, Park Superintendent E.P. Leavitt deemed it a "fire trap of the worst sort." In 1953, the NPS commissioned a report that recommended rehabilitation of the lodge: the cost, $72,000. Price balked at the recommendation and sold the concession to Harry Smith and his son the following year.

In 1959, the concession and building again changed hands, to Ralph Peyton and James Griffin. The NPS wanted to buy the lodge and either convert it into a visitor center and museum or demolish it. The concessionaire would then take the money and build a motel to accommodate guests. Finally, in 1967, the NPS bought the lodge as part of getting Peyton and Griffin to sign a thirty-year contract. For nearly

twenty years, the lodge opened each summer amid mounting problems and controversy.

In 1980, a General Accounting Office report criticized not only the lodge's safety problems, but also the drop in the number of overnight visitors. The next year, the lodge was added to the National Register of Historic Places, making changes or demolition a historic preservation issue. In 1984, following two decades of safety reports and studies, the National Park Service recommended demolishing the lodge and constructing a new hotel away from the rim. After surviving decades of brutal winter storms, sheltering thousands of visitors, enduring the indignities of "cosmetic" renovation and neglect, Crater Lake Lodge was in danger of being razed.

The truth was that the old lodge was a dump. The roof sagged, the bathrooms were spartan, light fixtures dangled from the ceiling, and wind whipped through the walls. From a distance, it had the appearance of a great lodge. But up close, it was a hodgepodge of neglect—an elegant idea that was never completed, but periodically patched up.

"The lodge was a pretty old building," recalled Michael Peyton, who spent his summers there while his father managed the lodge. "As time went by, it would kind of move and creak and groan with the snow in the winter. And it was getting so heavy on the roof that it was kind of flattening out the building and the walls were bowing."

Or more simply put: "It was a decrepit old derelict. It was in really sorry shape," summed up John Miele, Park Management Assistant for

the National Park Service at Crater Lake. Miele arrived at the park in 1985, and one of his first tasks was to assess the "issue" of the lodge.

The idea of losing Crater Lake Lodge struck many as unthinkable. Historic preservationists and nostalgia-driven Oregonians organized. Saving Crater Lake Lodge became a cause to be reckoned with. In 1984, the Historic Preservation League of Oregon officially began lobbying National Park Service about plans for the decrepit lodge.

Eric Eiseman, the league's director, launched a statewide campaign: "We ended up with over 4,000 testimonials, post cards, letters flooding into the office from people telling us about their experiences at the lodge and why those experiences were important in their lives. So, armed with that information, we went back to the National Park Service and said: 'Look at this unanimous support'."

The league challenged government reports and cost estimates for renovation in a position paper and began the fight. By 1987, the Oregon legislature passed a resolution to save the lodge.

"I think all of us have a share in a common heritage, and that heritage is our natural resources base and it's also an historic resource base. And that's why Crater Lake Lodge is such an important place, because it's part of our birthright that needs protecting," explained Eiseman.

During the fight, the lodge continued to decay, and a report completed by consulting engineers in 1989 suggested that the middle section, including the great hall and guest rooms on the upper floors, might collapse of its own weight. Park Service Regional Director Charles Odegaard ordered the lodge closed on May 26, 1989.

This was not the beginning of the end, but a respite before the lodge's transformation. Only two years after Crater Lake Lodge's closure, reconstruction began.

The rehabilitated four-story structure, with its forest-green roof and brown-shingled siding, built on a steel-reinforced foundation of native volcanic stone, is a reminder of the past. The historical architects working on the project had to look at the design in a new light. Instead of a traditional historic restoration, this would be a combination of reconstruction, rehabilitation, and restoration, to evoke the feeling of what the lodge should have been. The Portland architectural firm of Fletcher Farr Ayotte, whose original assignment was to design a new lodge, switched gears.

"With most historic structures there is usually an event, a person or an architectural style which defines its historic significance. Crater Lake Lodge had none of those," explained David Wark, the firm's lead architect on the project. "What it did have was a history that came from people's emotional attachment."

Miele echoed, "…a tremendous emotional attachment and affection between the people that have stayed here over the years and Crater Lake Lodge." Making the leap from "emotional attachment" to how to approach the project was the challenge.

After the firm's initial investigation, the first mystery to Wark was how the lodge was standing up. There were no foundations under the stone walls, and the mortar had turned to sand.

Huge cables anchored on steel plates at the front and the back of the lodge and installed after World War II held the building together. "When you had a heavy snow load, these cables were just as taunt as a fiddle string," said Miele. "In the summertime, the lodge would relax with the snow off, and the cable would be real loose."

The deeper the firm looked, the worse things got, with all of the structural systems in failure. The initial rehabilitation plan became one of partial reconstruction. "And so our strategy was to keep as much as the original fabric, remove it, and then put it back after we had installed new systems," said Wark.

Besides the structural problems, there was the interior. A reception desk blocked lake views, a gift shop with fluorescent light fixtures dominated the great hall space, dining room décor included tacky wine casks and bug zappers, layers of carpeting (twenty-two different types were identified) covered the floors, and uninviting guestrooms had gaps between the walls. All of the rooms were furnished in what Wark called "bad Sixties furniture—the primary material was Naugahyde."

At least the main floor hadn't always been that way, and historical photographs gave a blueprint to the rustic lodge simplicity that had long ago lost its dignity.

On May 1, 1991, Phase I began. Crews began to dismantle the great hall. Stone walls were taken apart, and fireplace stones numbered for reconstruction. New foundations were poured, then a steel-beamed infrastructure was constructed, and carpenters framed the great hall. A Herculean body of work readied the skeleton for the aging skin of stone and wood to cover. The new great hall served as an anchor around which the rest of the rehabilitation was done. All of the exterior walls, except the great hall, are a facade of original materials. The kitchen was gutted and replaced.

Stones that framed windows and doors were saved and put back in their original places. What was not replaced was reconfigured in the same rough character. The huge exterior stairway was removed. All entries or exits had

Seating areas in the great hall create inviting places to relax, facing page, but the veranda off the back of the lodge is the most popular spot from which to enjoy lake views, above.

The great hall demolition and reconstruction recreated a lodge that William Steel once dreamed of, left. Seen from the lakeside, below, the rebuilt lodge stands as a reminder of the park's cultural history.

to be incorporated into existing doors. Sixty-hour weeks were the norm, with winter breathing down the workers' necks. When construction was halted for the season, a centerpiece had been created.

Phase II lasted three summers. While the centerpiece was well underway, the unstable annex and annex wing were shored up and stabilized with new foundations and support columns. All of the reconstruction had to meet seismic guidelines. The entire roof was replaced, including rafters and cedar shingles.

This time, they built a lodge that could hold not only memories, but also withstand the tons of snow that pile on the rooftop and the thirty-foot drifts that bank the walls.

While exterior work continued, attention turned to the interior. That began at the entry. "There was no sense of arrival in the original design," noted Wark, "no orientation to the lake." Seeing the lake—the very reason for the lodge's existence—became the hallmark for interior plans and design.

The stone fireplaces in the dining room and great hall anchored interior rehabilitation. "Each stone was numbered and put back exactly as they were," explained Wark. "The interior log paneling are segments of large logs that were cut and placed as finish material in the lobby and dining room."

The great hall's thirteen-foot-high beamed ceiling was redone, hardwood floors laid and polished, geometric designs cut in the linoleum floor entry, and the dining room restored to its original charm complete with Crater Lake Lodge china on the tables. Guestrooms were reconfigured to accommodate private bathrooms, some with clawfoot tubs. And while modern amenities were added, no telephones or televisions are present in the rooms. A new menu was devised featuring

Northwest cuisine and the wine list fine-tuned.

The new décor blends Stickley reproductions, Mission, metal, and log-and-twig furniture and accessories. The lobby and great hall, with intimate furniture groupings, were readied for guests to lounge, play cards, talk, or simply relax.

After six years and $15 million of painstaking renovation, on May 20, 1995, Crater Lake Lodge reopened. Fifteen to twenty feet of snow still covered the landscape, but guests were not deterred. Visitors filled the seventy-one perfectly appointed rooms in hopes of recapturing memories of honeymoons and family vacations.

Russell Sadler, who first came to the lodge in 1965 for a summer job as wine steward, was there: "Where else can you spend the night on the edge of a caldera made by a mighty eruption over seven thousand years ago, and contemplate the sunset and sunrise?" He paused to take in the always-changing scene. "I mean, there aren't very many places like this."

Crater Lake Lodge, the elegant idea of another era, was finally a reality. The architects, historians, contractors, and designers took nostalgia and a decaying old lodge and gave them new life. As one historian noted, "It's glorified history—history without the smells."

David Wark specializes in historic building work, but Crater Lake Lodge and its renewal were often about people: "Having a role in a building that connects with people and this unique environment, and to bring back that connection is, for me, what made it all a very challenging and rewarding project."

The essence of Crater Lake Lodge lies in its memories. While the historic structure no longer bears the ragged signs of aging, the heart of the lodge remains the same. It is still a wonder of man perched on the edge of a wonder of nature.

The rubble stone walls, bark-covered log columns, and linen-covered tables look much the same as when the lodge opened in 1915.

CRATER LAKE NATIONAL PARK

ONE OF NATURE'S MAJESTIC SURPRISES

Crater Lake is a visual gift, a sensory experience. Surrounded by a fringe of hemlock, pine and fir, it lies hidden in what was once a massive mountain peak. You walk to the edge, and the sight is sprung upon you.

Crater Lake National Park celebrates its centennial in 2002 with no need for party favors. Each trail, each vista, each extravagant scene transformed with the changing light is a gift we can all treasure.

The only national park in Oregon, this patch of geologic wonder is a relatively compact covering layer of basalt, andesite, and pumice.

That volcanic story is the crux of Crater Lake National Park, and park rangers like interpreter Kevin Bacher share the story with visitors. One of the best places to hear the saga is from the lake. No private boats are allowed on the water, but concession-operated excursions are offered through the summer season.

An intrepid group of park visitors has hiked down the steep trail at Cleetwood Cove to a dock on the water's edge. They hand over their tickets and climb aboard one of the fifty-foot-long wooden vessels as tourists have done since 1907.

As the boat chugs across the water, they gaze up the caldera walls that can reach 1,980 feet. Park Ranger Bacher begins his story. "The eruption that formed the lake 7,700 years ago was epic, one of the largest to occur in this part of the world for tens if not hundreds of thousands of years," he explains of the blast that blew ash and pumice over what would become eight states and three Canadian provinces.

Eventually, the whole structure of the mountain failed, cracks began to form in a ring around the edge of the mountain, and the peak collapsed, leaving a huge basin. Over time, snow and rain filled the caldera, creating Crater Lake.

Hidden below its surrounding rim, Crater Lake is one of nature's great surprises, facing page. Wildlife is abundant, right, as are the vantage points from which to view the lake and Wizard Island rising out of the deep blue water.

Skell of the Above World, who became pitted in a battle that resulted in the destruction of Llao's home, Mount Mazama. That massive destruction created Crater Lake.

"The story told in the language of legend is consistent with the story told in the language of geology that you see here today," continues Bacher.

The boat passes Phantom Ship, a jagged piece of volcanic rock protruding from the water. Sights also include Pumice Castle, Llao Rock, Devils Backbone, and Wizard Island where passengers can get off the boat and spend the day exploring the cinder cone. Bacher searches for Old Man of the Lake, a hemlock log that floats upright and travels with the lake's wind and currents. "There he is," someone shouts as the log end bobs in the icy water.

The caldera spans more than six miles at its widest point, and sonar surveys have calculated its maximum depth at 1,958 feet. The intense blue color of the lake is attributed to its clarity and depth. There are no inlets, and rain and snow fill the caldera while evaporation and seepage keep it in balance.

From the time John Wesley Hillman called it the bluest lake he had ever seen, people have been taken aback by the color. That blue is created as the pure water absorbs the reds, yellows, and greens of sunlight leaving behind the blue that so permanently impresses everyone who sees it. But the lake is not an endless azure waterscape. Soon after the collapse, minor eruptions created formations like Wizard Island.

The boat tour is by no means the only way to experience the park. Crater Lake is the park's magnet, but geologic wonders abound beyond its namesake.

By mid-July, when the snow has finally been cleared, a thirty-three-mile road that first opened in 1940 offers a route around the rim.

On this tour, Bacher points out evidence that scientists have used to understand what happened at this mountain: layers of rock exposed in the caldera wall and remnants of volcanic peaks scattered around the lake.

"Scientists also had the advantage here at Crater Lake of the stories that have been told by people in this area for thousands of years," explains Bacher. "We know that people have lived here in the Crater Lake area for 10,000 years, maybe much longer, because of archaeological evidence unearthed especially in the Klamath Basin."

There are many versions of the Mount Mazama legend, but the Klamath people's story tells of two chiefs, Llao of the Below World and

Rim Drive's two-hour trip holds dozens of pullouts with magnificent views of the lake. One side road off Rim Drive on the east side of the lake takes visitors to the Pinnacles Overlook, where interpretative stations explain how 7,700 years of erosion created this bizarre stand of hollow pumice spires.

For those who enjoy hiking, 140 miles of trails open up a world of wildflowers, forests of hemlock and red fir, grassy meadows, springs, canyons, and mountaintop vistas. More than fifty types of mammals make their home at the park, including snowshoe hares, mule deer, Roosevelt elk, bobcats, and a few dozen black bears. The northern spotted owl and American bald eagles are among the species in the park listed as "threatened" under the Endangered Species Act.

The park's historic architecture is a chapter in its cultural story. Crater Lake Lodge is located at Rim Village on the south side of the caldera, and three miles south of that is park headquarters with the historic administrative offices, ranger station, visitor center and staff housing, many part of a current historic rehabilitation project.

Mazama Village, seven miles south of Rim Village, is the site of the park's major campground, camp store, and motor lodge.

Although the Crater Lake Lodge is closed from mid-October to the end of May, the park is open year-round, and cross-country skiers and snowshoers—undaunted by over 500 inches of snow that falls each winter—revel in the beauty.

Still, it is the lake in the summer that is the park's main draw. Today, 500,000 visitors come each year, step to the edge of the rim, and take in the wonder of it all.

Phantom Ship peeks from the depths of the lake, facing page. Guided boat tours take visitors through Skell Channel by Wizard Island, below. Sights like the Pinnacles, right, illustrate the park's geologic variety.

CANYON COUNTRY

On the north and south rims of the Grand Canyon, and in the colorful formations of Utah's Zion and Bryce Canyon national parks are a series of lodges designed by master architects, some altered by fire, yet each finding a comfortable fit in settings that humble them.

El Tovar is both an elegant European retreat and an American log cabin, above. The 1904 photograph shows the hotel near completion, facing page.

EL TOVAR

OPENED 1905

The historic Grand Canyon Railway chugs through piñon, juniper woodlands, ponderosa pines, and the open range of the Coconino Plateau as it makes its way from Williams, Arizona, to the South Rim of the Grand Canyon. Cattle, antelope and deer scatter as the diesel engine pulls its cargo of sightseers that fill the restored Pullman cars. The scenery along the line may seem rather ordinary, but it is the perfect build-up, a two-hour-and-fifteen-minute tease for what is to come. If Yosemite and Yellowstone national parks' treasures barrage the senses, the Grand Canyon is simply a heart-stopper.

On September 17, 1901, Engine 282 pulled the first passenger train up to the South Rim.

A century later, restored Engine 6793 backs into the historic Grand Canyon Depot at the South Rim. Passengers pour out of the cars. Some board tour buses, but others climb the forty-two steps from the log depot toward El Tovar. They glance at the hotel to their left and Hopi House across the plaza, but continue straight ahead.

"It is not until the sightseer reaches the edge that the full force of the view strikes him with a shock that makes him gasp," exclaimed a 1905 Santa Fe Railway brochure.

Some things never change.

"It's a sound people make. It's not a word, but a gut level 'oomph'," interpretive ranger Ron Brown explained. "A visceral reaction. I hear that sound a lot."

Formed by the erosive powers of the Colorado River over a period of 5 million years, the canyon's layer upon layer of geologic history plummets below. Visitors peer down the 5,000-foot crevice and across the ten-mile span. For a moment, they stand in respectful silence, their first words often voiced in a whisper.

After being momentarily sated by sight of the canyon, they turn to the rambling hotel. No one gasps at the sight of El Tovar.

Instead of constructing an obtrusive monument to man and the railway, architect Charles Whittlesey saw an opportunity to create another layer upon this remarkable canvas. When El Tovar is caught in the late-day sun, golden rays

wash it with the same rich hues that bathe the canyon below. The low-slung stone, wood, and log hotel—with its varied rooflines—seems to sink into the landscape.

For most visitors, El Tovar is a not-to-be missed stop on the canyon tour. To others, it is a legacy. Andrew Whittlesey never knew his grandfather, Charles, but he and his family are drawn to the hotel: "It's something very magical. It seems to transcend that era. Something so out of context yet blending into the southwestern architecture. It spans several cultures and comes together at that one special point."

Part Victorian-era resort and part rustic log cabin when it opened in 1905, it provided both the comforts of the established Eastern or European resorts and the excitement of the newly "discovered" Southwest.

"Folks were on this western adventure at the end of the line—literally the end of the line—and they had this wonderful lodge to greet them. I look at El Tovar as of another place that is transposed simply because its style is so unlike that of the Grand Canyon, but as a building, as a

GRANDE DAME OF THE SOUTH RIM
GRAND CANYON NATIONAL PARK, ARIZONA

lodge, it is beautiful. Add to that the railroad history, and it works," said Jan Balsom, the park's chief of cultural resource programs. "El Tovar, it's just an icon."

The region's human history began long before tourists arrived. Zuni, Hopi, Navajo, Havasupai, Hualapai, and Southern Paiute tribes lived, farmed, hunted, and built their homes and pueblos in the semi-arid Southwest perhaps 10,000 years ago. Spanish conquistadors, led by Francisco Vásquez de Coronado, were the first Europeans to lead an expedition into what is now the American Southwest. Their quest for the fabled Seven Cities of Cibola failed, but stories of a great river intrigued Coronado. He dispatched García Lopez de Cárdenas to find the river that cut through the seemingly barren landscape. Cárdenas, with Hopi guides, is credited as the first white man to view the Grand Canyon in 1540. Cárdenas may have been impressed, but he was not in search of staggering beauty—rather, a route to the Gulf of California. Thwarted by the massive obstacle, he returned to Mexico City.

Spanish missionary Francisco Tomás Garcés viewed the Grand Canyon somewhere near the South Rim in 1776. Mexico secured its independence from New Spain in 1821, and the canyon remained the territory of Mexico from then until the end of the Mexican-American War in 1848. Two years later, the Territory of New Mexico, which included the Grand Canyon, was created.

Trappers and traders were familiar with the region, but the three most significant expeditions into the Grand Canyon began in 1868 under the leadership of Major John Wesley Powell. His work not only provided the first real information on the uncharted territory, but also introduced its mysteries to the American public.

Colorful posters and brochures filled with superlatives about the Grand Canyon and its facilities were part of the Santa Fe's marketing of the national park.

Naturalist and conservationist John Muir traveled to the canyon and called it "God's spectacle," while naturalist John Burroughs described it as the "divine abyss."

The canyon had evolved from an obstacle to a wonder and would become a potential opportunity. Miners put aside their picks and began catering to the budding tourist trade. Small hotels and cabins, served by stage lines, were the first tourist accommodations. Early tourists to the Grand Canyon stayed at the Grandview

Hotel, built in 1895 eleven miles east of what is now Grand Canyon Village, and Bright Angel Hotel and tent camp, built soon after.

Like other railways at the turn of the 20th century, the Atchison, Topeka & Santa Fe was opening up tourism in exotic American landscapes. The Santa Fe Railway acquired a bankrupt train line from Williams to Anita Junction, Arizona, and completed the spur to Grand Canyon Village with the intent of using it for copper mining. Copper may not have panned out, but passengers did. They arrived on the Santa Fe's intercontinental line and transferred at Williams onto The Grand Canyon Railway, whose trains departed regularly for Grand Canyon Village.

The train and tourists arrived at a destination ripe for first class development. Railway officials saw the success of rival Northern Pacific's interests at Yellowstone National Park, and they projected even more visitors to the panoramic vistas of the Grand Canyon—a region that could accommodate tourists year round. The Northern Pacific's Old Faithful Inn opened in June 1904, and the Santa Fe's El Tovar welcomed its first guests seven months later.

As with most of the West, preservation and exploitation ran neck and neck. President Benjamin Harrison secured the Grand Canyon Forest Reserve in 1893, but it would be nearly three decades before the stunning reaches of the Grand Canyon got full national park status.

President Theodore Roosevelt's 1903 visit to the Grand Canyon gave the American people an idea of just what that huge chasm in the seemingly barren high desert of Arizona was all about: "In the Grand Canyon, Arizona has a natural wonder which, so far as I know, is in kind absolutely unparalleled throughout the rest of the world."

The first passengers arrived at the South Rim in 1901, upper right. Today, tourists board the restored trains at Williams, above, and chug through the landscape, right, before arriving at the Grand Canyon Depot with El Tovar reigning above it, top.

In 1906, Roosevelt created the Grand Canyon Game Reserve by executive order. That same year, he signed the Antiquities Act, which gave him legislative authority to establish Grand Canyon National Monument two years later. He also enlarged the Forest Reserve into a National Forest, all before Arizona statehood in 1912. By the time the Grand Canyon became a national park in 1919 during the presidency of Woodrow Wilson, the South Rim already had been developed, and the Santa Fe's El Tovar reigned as the flagship hotel of Grand Canyon Village.

And what a hotel it was!

Newspaper accounts speculated that "The building itself will be worth a trip to the canyon," and the architecture was described as a combination of "Swiss chateaux" and "castles of the Rhine." Even with its shingle-wrapped turret (water storage tank) and elegant interior solariums and lounges, it evoked the mood of the West that the Santa Fe was promoting.

The combination of cultures was not by chance; architect Charles Whittlesey, who was trained in the Chicago office of Louis Sullivan, and who had designed other hotels and stations on the Santa Fe line, saw an opportunity to meld the elegance of a European villa with the informality of a hunting lodge. Initial plans called for a more modest hotel, but by May 1902, the *Coconino Sun* reported that Whittlesey had been instructed to double the size of the hotel.

Dubbed Bright Angel Tavern during the planning stages, its name was changed before opening to the more suitable El Tovar Hotel, in keeping with the Santa Fe's tradition of naming

its hotels of the region after Spanish explorers. The Santa Fe had already named its Trinidad, Colorado, hotel after Cárdenas, so Pedro de Tobar received the honor.

Tobar never actually got to the South Rim of the canyon with the Coronado expedition. No matter, the "b" in his name was changed to a

An American flag was draped on the wall of the Rendezvous Room for this 1906 photograph, above. Today, the Rendezvous Room retains its rusticity, facing page.

"v" (the antique Spanish spelling also eliminated the possible mispronunciation of "to-the-bar" that the Santa Fe feared).

The Santa Fe's Montezuma Hot Springs Hotel "spa" resort outside of Las Vegas had been plagued with problems. Two fires and a dwindling clientele prompted the railway to reevaluate its future, and focus on the Grand Canyon project.

"The staff was brought over from the Montezuma—from general manager to bell hops—and given a month or two to get it ready to handle tourists," explained Gordon Chappell, National Park Service (NPS) senior historian.

The grand hotel was officially named and opened on January 14, 1905. Its opening doubled the number of guestrooms available at Grand Canyon Village.

Steam heat, electric lights and indoor plumbing all made it "the most expensively constructed and appointed log house in America." Huge Douglas-firs were shipped by rail from Oregon, pushing the cost of the hotel to $250,000, a grand sum, especially when compared to Old Faithful Inn, built for $140,000. One hundred guestrooms accommodated visitors who found comfort in "a quiet dignity, an unassuming luxury, and an appreciation of outing needs" at El Tovar.

That sense of "dignity and luxury" remains today. "There's a feeling of pride and elegance when you see it. There's something about the building that says, 'This is the place'," according to Dennis Reason, who has worked at the Grand Canyon since 1980. "It's the premier spot on the rim, and it deserves to be there. It may be the gem of the canyon now, but in 1905 it had to have been the gem of the West."

In 1909-1910, the railway built the train station (designed by Santa Barbara architect Francis Wilson) just below the hotel. Large copper letters spelling out "Grand Canyon" were placed under the gable of the log depot. Guests arrived at the platform and looked up at

the solariums, rooftop porches with ten-foot posts topped with trefoils, and the turret of El Tovar— the European castle. Then they proceeded up the steps to the main entrance and ascended onto the veranda. Log beams and columns, mission-style stone corner walls with arched openings, and a gable roof, all evoked El Tovar's other personality: the log cabin.

Log slabs sheathed the dining, kitchen and utility wing, extending the cabin image, while gazebos off the north porch were finished with jigsawn patterns reminiscent of a Swiss chalet. A much-loved quote from C.A. Higgins' booklet *Titan of Chasms* appears on the lintel above the porch: "Dreams of mountains, as in their sleep they brood on things eternal."

Inside, El Tovar offers old-world charm along with a heavy dose of rusticity. Stepping through the entrance one enters the Rendezvous Room where dark-stained log-slab walls, exposed log rafters, and a corner stone fireplace surround the forty-one-by-thirty-seven-foot space.

"On the upper shelf repose heads of the deer, elk, moose, mountain sheep, and buffalo, mingling with curiously shaped, and gaudily-tinted Indian jars from the Southwest pueblos," a 1909 brochure described the scene. The furniture was Arts and Crafts design, some later identified as Gustav Stickley. "Nothing cheap nor tawdry is tolerated," boasted the brochure.

In the center of the building is the registration lobby, or Rotunda, where "all paths intersect." The log-fronted registration desk has changed little, and the mezzanine lounge above it has an octagonal balcony with Swiss-styled jigsawn balustrades. This was the crimson-draped Ladies Lounge where "…the better half of the world may see without being seen—may chat and gossip—may sew and read—may do any of the inconsequent nothings which serve to pleasantly pass the time away."

On March 17, 1911, President Theodore Roosevelt led a group into the canyon, left. Due to his perseverance, two years later it became a national park. When visiting the canyon, Roosevelt often took his meals at El Tovar's private dining room, below.

Peter Werdermann has worked from his desk in the Rotunda for a decade. As El Tovar's concierge he has seen people from all walks of life: "All the famous people will visit the Grand Canyon, and everybody will come and look at the great old house. They all smile. They think it's just a wonderful place."

Part of the draw of El Tovar was and remains the dining room. Elegant meals, prepared by an "Italian chef, once employed in New York and Chicago clubs," were served in the eighty-nine-foot-long dining room, where the famed "Harvey Girls" waited tables. The kitchen of El Tovar has always prepared notable cuisine. A herd of Jersey cows and a poultry farm supplied fresh milk, butter, and eggs. The hotel had its own bakery, butcher shop, and bulk storage refrigerators to keep Pacific salmon, California fruit, Kansas beef, and imported cheeses.

The huge dining room (three times the size of the Rendezvous Room) has two stone chimneys, each flanked by large picture windows. Four large murals by Brue Himeche depict the customs of four Indian tribes: the Hopi, Apache, Mojave, and Navajo. The simple Arts and Crafts period chairs and tables are only seen in historic photos. Stained-glass lights now hang instead of the original log chandeliers. A side porch was converted to the Canyon Dining Room, where a 1920 Chris Jorgenson painting hangs opposite the bank of windows facing the rim. Porches along the dining room were later additions.

A richly paneled, private dining room was (and still is) available for intimate dinners. The story goes that the room was specifically added for Teddy Roosevelt, who liked to show up for dinner in his muddy boots and riding gear.

The Santa Fe Railway alone was not responsible for the success of El Tovar. The Fred Harvey Company managed the hotel, along with

The elegant main dining room, originally furnished with Arts and Crafts style furniture, has always been known for its excellent cuisine.

other railway properties. Fred Harvey had opened his first restaurant at the Santa Fe Depot in Topeka, Kansas, in 1876, before the addition of dining cars to trains. What followed was a thriving business with restaurants built by the railway along the Santa Fe lines through Colorado, Kansas, Texas, New Mexico, Arizona, California, and Alabama, and managed by Fred Harvey.

Food and service were foremost, and the

waitresses began working in 1883. The hard working, well trained, and strictly chaperoned young women drew quite a following. (In the 1940s, Metro-Goldwyn-Mayer released a musical, *The Harvey Girls,* starring Judy Garland, Angela Lansbury, and Preston Wills.)

The senior Harvey died in 1901 before El Tovar opened, but his sons continued managing the South Rim facilities, purchasing them from the Santa Fe in 1954. The Fred Harvey Com-

Part of the railway's advertising included commissioning artists to capture scenes such as Louis Akin's 1907 painting El Tovar Hotel, top. That painting included the Mary Colter designed Hopi House, above, where Indian crafts were made and displayed.

pany became a subsidiary of AmFac, Inc., in 1968.

The Santa Fe Railway and Fred Harvey Company together blazed a new trail in advertising and marketing merchandise in conjunction with their train lines, stations, and destination facilities. They introduced images of the Southwest, and Indian arts—jewelry, rugs, and basketry—to the rest of the country at world fairs and expositions, as well as in retail concerns. The Santa Fe hired and promoted artists and photographers, including Thomas Moran, to capture the beauty of the Southwest.

Expositions were the rage, and the Santa Fe and the Fred Harvey Company took full advantage of the venues to bring the Southwest to the masses. Their efforts for the 1915 San Francisco Panama-Pacific International Exposition were grandiose if not as grand as the canyon itself. "The Grand Canyon of Arizona" six-acre exhibit included an Indian village plus a replica of the canyon to be viewed from cars that carried tourists along the "rim" for twenty-five cents a trip.

Under the direction of the railway's general advertising agent, William Simpson, the company acquired a vast art collection and became a corporate patron of the arts. Included was the 1907 Louis Akin painting "El Tovar Hotel, Grand Canyon." As early as 1902, the Indian Department of the Fred Harvey Company began collecting Native American art and artifacts to sell in its shops and to use for decorating.

The Santa Fe and the Harvey Company strove to monopolize the South Rim's "entertainment." Guests wanted more than to view the canyon from the rim, but others had already built trails where they guided trips. The Santa Fe's solution was to acquire access, then construct a trail and road of its own. "Trail Drives and Saddle Horses" were advertised in their 1912 brochures. The hotel provided divided skirts for the women and leggings for the men if they were not prepared for the ride.

The railway brought more than tourists and supplies to the park. During its heyday, when El Tovar needed to be reshingled, the railroad brought in a train of work and tool cars that housed the "B&B Gang," or Bridges and Buildings. When El Tovar needed repainting, a different train came in that housed the Paint Gang, and so on.

While early tourists embraced rail travel, by 1926 more visitors were arriving by private car than Pullman car. The historic depot closed in 1968, and El Tovar was showing serious signs of aging.

Beginning in 1975, major rehabilitation projects costing millions of dollars began to bring back the Grande Dame's lost dignity.

Over time the Solarium and Music Room were converted into some of the twelve guest suites, each individually decorated. Their history has not been forgotten; each suite bears a name from the past: Charles Whittlesey, Fred Harvey, Coronado, and Miss Colter's Study. As part of the décor, historic photos show the spaces as they were used at a time where leisurely afternoons were spent reading, writing, or listening to music. In addition, paintings by Phoenix artist James Knauf of the original scenes grace two of the suites.

El Tovar maintains the aristocratic atmosphere and Western intrigue it was intended to evoke as a destination for the elite. Part of that intrigue was with the Indian culture and art work. Hopi House, designed by Mary Colter, a onetime Minnesota drawing and design teacher, opened just prior to El Tovar. Built to replicate a Hopi pueblo, it was the perfect site for the Harvey collection of Navajo blankets.

Watchtower, Mary Colter's 1932 masterpiece, was patterned after ancient towers and kivas and decorated with Indian cave and wall drawings.

Indian artisans produced jewelry, pottery, blankets, and other artwork and trinkets for sale.

"There was nothing else out here in 1905, it was another day's journey to 'Indian land,' so right across the way from El Tovar is Hopi House—an adobe complete with the craftspeople—and the guests only had to walk across the plaza to experience the arts and crafts," noted Jan Balsom. "They didn't forget a detail. Absolutely everything, even the aged look of things, was planned. I look back on it, and it's amazing to me what they were able to do."

Hopi House was the first of a series of projects Colter produced as architect and interior designer for Fred Harvey Company. El Tovar was the compound's flagship, but Colter's design and decorating work fills the area. In 1914, Colter designed Hermits Rest along the Santa Fe's trail into the canyon. That same year, The Lookout Studio was built west of El Tovar as a canyon viewpoint and shop to sell postcards, photographs, and art work. Other Colter buildings at the Grand Canyon include: Phantom Ranch eight miles into the canyon, 1922; Watchtower, at the end of Desert View, 1932; Bright Angel Lodge, designed as an economy lodge with surrounding cabins to replace the original Bright Angel Camp, 1935; Men's Dormitory, 1936; and Women's Dormitory, 1937.

Grand Canyon Village, on the South Rim, was named a National Historic Landmark in 1997. There are ten such individual designations in the park, including El Tovar, Lookout Studio, Hopi House, Hermits Rest, and Watchtower, along with the Grand Canyon Depot, and Grand Canyon Lodge. Many others are on the National Register of Historic Places.

In 1989 the long abandoned Grand Canyon Railway line again began moving passengers from Williams to the South Rim. The train departs daily from historic 1908 Williams Depot—pulled by rebuilt steam locomotives in the summer, with 1950-vintage diesel engines for winter runs—and ends at Grand Canyon Depot beneath El Tovar.

Grand Canyon Village overflows with historic buildings, people, and activity. "Visitors are against a landscape that is too large to grasp in many ways, so the buildings provide that touchstone. That human touch, and I revel in it," said Jan Balsom. "You can easily imagine you've just taken the train, and you sit on the porch of El Tovar and feel what it was like in 1905."

GRAND CANYON NATIONAL PARK

THE DIVINE ABYSS

"How long does it take to see the Grand Canyon?" an interpretive sign reads at the new visitor center near Mather Point. "It takes anywhere from a moment to a life time," is the answer.

Mather Point, on a precipice along the South Rim, is one of the first spots where visitors view the canyon. NPS ranger Ron Brown watches the faces and listens to gasps, sighs, and silence as visitors tentatively step toward the rim. "It is not a fear of heights that strikes them, but the immensity of it all. It is a religious experience for many, trying to observe it, to take it all in."

When the moment is right, Ron Brown steps in to put the vastness of the place in perspective. "I point out a little patch of river that is the size of a football field or sixty-foot cottonwoods that look like dots. When they realize that little blue line is a building, they can put it into context." Studying birds of prey brought Brown to the Grand Canyon, and from Mather Point he studies their migrations. "Not counting Texas, this is the best place in the world to watch birds of prey. Over 6,000 birds a year fly over Yaki and Mather points. This is profoundly impressive."

Even more impressive is the view from this point, with a scene that plummets 5,000 feet below to the Colorado River and stretches as far as the eye can see, yet encompasses only seventeen percent of the 1,218,376-acre park. The canyon's crevice lays open the story of geologic time. Within each layer of exposed canyon wall are sandwiched intervals of the earth's history. The newest layer of 250-million-year-old Kaibab limestone tops the rim, with 2-billion-year-old rocks of the Inner Gorge still being cut by the Colorado River as it roars through 277 miles of the park's canyon floor. While the rocks may be in the billion-year-old category, the canyon itself is relatively young. Most geolo-

gists feel that the canyon formed within the last five million years.

The variety of rock layers and each one's reaction to erosion creates the magnificent colors and formations that give the "divine abyss" its vast texture and complexity. Iron and other minerals cause the colors that are changed and intensified as the sunlight and clouds play upon this palette. Sunrises and sunsets should not be missed.

Grand Canyon can be looked at as three distinct parks: the South Rim and Grand Canyon Village, where most visitors stay; the canyon floor where campsites and the Mary Colter-designed Phantom Ranch offer overnight shelter; and the less accessible and higher North Rim that opens each May and closes in October. Each offers its own experience.

Today, a free shuttle service takes visitors to popular spots along the South Rim. Greenways, for bike and foot traffic, along with a future light rail or bus system, are changing the way you visit the park. An excellent way to plan your trip is to stop at the Canyon View Visitor Center where you'll find a stunning new complex of buildings using sustainable architecture and construction techniques.

Tourists at the turn of the 20th century wanted to explore the inner canyon, as do travelers of the 21st century. A trip to the bottom of the canyon and back (on foot or by mule) takes two days. Rim-to-rim hikers generally spend three days to get from the North Rim to the South Rim. (It is a five-hour drive from the South to the North Rim of the park.) A trip through Grand Canyon by raft can take two weeks or longer, and there are those who spend weeks exploring the park's wilderness.

In 1919, the first year that Grand Canyon was a national park, 44,173 visitors came to see the latest addition to America's national park

Watons Throne rises 7,633 feet, and is seen here from Cape Royal on the canyon North Rim, facing page. The sun rises over the horizon at Hopi Point on the South Rim, above.

system. By 1956, visitorship passed the 1 million mark, and in 1969 over 2 million tourists came to the park. In 1998, nearly 5 million people visited the park.

Besides the huge influx of tourists and staff, eighty-eight species of mammals, 287 different birds, twenty-five kinds of fishes, and fifty species of reptiles and amphibians call the park home. The full range of vegetation varies from the spruce-fir-aspen forest of the North Rim to the desert at the bottom of the canyon. Cacti are found throughout much of that range—except at high elevations—and not only in the "desert."

Early problems of roaming cattle, sewage disposal, and lack of zoning were periodically

Early morning light plays off the canyon walls from Hopi Point, left. The canyon panorama includes smaller details such as the rock formations near Yaki Point, facing page.

replaced with new challenges that came with the growth and development of Grand Canyon Village. By 1924, the NPS and Santa Fe Railway devised a master plan for developing the South Rim, the most traveled portion of the park. Since then it has been a work in progress.

In 1995 the Grand Canyon National Park General Management Plan was approved. It was the culmination of a four-year process that involved local citizens, American Indian tribes, and public and private agencies.

The plan is just that—a plan—to guide the resource management, visitor use, and general development at the park over a ten- to fifteen-year period with the goal of protecting while providing meaningful visitor experiences. A secondary purpose is to encourage compatible activities on adjacent lands so as to minimize negative effects on the park.

On January 11, 2000, on the ninety-second anniversary of President Teddy Roosevelt's designation of the Grand Canyon as a national monument, President Bill Clinton signed proclamations giving monument status to some of those adjoining lands. As he stood at the North Rim, he said, "What a remarkable place this canyon is. It is in so many ways the symbol of our great natural expanse, our beauty and our spirit."

The stone columns of Zion Park Lodge, above circa 1930, were incorporated in the second set of drawings done by architect Gilbert Stanley Underwood, facing page.

ZION PARK LODGE

OPENED 1925

As the 20th century began, the southern environs of Utah and its panoramas of shifting colors and eroded landscape had been overlooked in America's quest for Western adventure. By 1905, the South Rim of the Grand Canyon had a bustling tourist trade that was a boon to the Santa Fe Railway. Now, the possibility of promoting tourism in the colorful canyons of southern Utah seemed to have potential for the state, federal government, and Union Pacific railroad.

The stunning region still was virtually inaccessible. Native peoples had hunted game and gathered wild plants and seeds, later building pueblos and planting crops. Fur trappers and traders blazed the Old Spanish Trail, which followed a portion of the Virgin River. By the time John Wesley Powell arrived in 1872 as part of western survey conducted by the U.S. Geological Survey, Mormon settlers were there to greet him. Having pushed south of Salt Lake City pursuing cotton-growing land in Utah's "Dixie," they had settled in Zion Canyon, establishing the town of Springdale in 1862. Powell chose Mukuntuweap, "straight river," as the canyon's name. The Mormon community found "Zion" more fitting.

Farming was a struggle, but there was no denying the splendor of the setting. When talk came of the area becoming part of a national monument, the Mormon settlers agreed. In 1909,

Mukuntuweap National Monument was established, and that same year the Utah State Road Commission began constructing a highway system to unlock the beauty of southern Utah.

As with other scenic destinations in America, it would be a railroad that first transported the public to these spectacular destinations. The Union Pacific's Los Angeles/Salt Lake City main line stopped at Lund, Utah, north of the monument, where a few hardy tourists left the comfort of their Pullman cars and boarded coaches for the country that would later be called "A Colorful Kingdom of Scenic Splendor." The "Kingdom's" accommodations consisted of campsites at the mouth of Zion Canyon, the North Rim of the Grand Canyon (operated by the Wylie brothers), and on the rim of Bryce Canyon. Even with primitive shelter and rocky roads, the touring public was enthralled by this remarkable country.

Horace Albright, acting superintendent of the National Park Service, began transforming the region into a group of national parks and monuments. As Stephen Mather's right-hand-man in charge during one of Mather's illnesses, Albright first looked over the southern Utah canyonlands' national park potential in 1917. The fledgling National Park Service had its hands full with developing Yellowstone, Yosemite, and Mount Rainier national parks, but Mather agreed that national park status was the only way to assure preservation of the divine landscapes that included Zion and Bryce canyons. Mukuntuweap National Monument was renamed Zion National Monument in 1918. In 1919, Zion National Monument came into the national park fold.

"They, Albright and Mather, both knew that if people didn't visit these places they wouldn't value these places," explained Tom Haraden, assistant chief naturalist at Zion National Park. "They were the right people for the right time, and that doesn't happen very often. If they weren't doing what they did when they did it, we wouldn't have what we have today."

With few funds to develop park tourist facilities, Mather turned to the Union Pacific railroad. The UP system saw potential in extending railroad lines into the little known and commercially untouched portion of Utah. Not only would the lines open up the spectacular red and white canyons of Zion and pink lime-

THE FIRST "LOOP TOUR" LODGE
ZION NATIONAL PARK, UTAH

stone formations of Bryce to tourism, they also would provide transportation lines for agricultural products, coal, and ore from the region.

In late 1922, the Union Pacific outlined a five-million-dollar plan that included constructing a new road from Lund to Cedar City, and creating lodging for the Cedar City, Zion and Bryce sites and a smaller facility at Cedar Breaks (made a national monument in 1933). The UP would later include Grand Canyon Lodge on the North Rim and the Kaibab Forest in what it called the "Loop Tour" to "The most colorful vacation region on earth!" via motor coaches.

Once the UP settled on the tour concept, challenges for completing the project were huge. Road access to the parks, forests and monuments was miserable, and the water situation unreliable. After securing concession contracts to the parks and monument areas and confirmation that the roads would be improved, the UP constructed a branch rail line from Lund to Cedar City, where a new depot was built; in 1923, they opened El Escalante Hotel in Cedar City, the "Gateway to the Utah Parks."

Stephen Mather, aware of the railway's obvious domination of the development, required that a separate company be formed to manage the operation. Utah Parks Company (UPC), a railroad subsidiary, was established for appearance's sake.

The first major construction was Zion Park Lodge. Initially, the plan was to build at the site of the Wylie Camp. Instead, a spot with a spectacular canyon view, and better airflow and motor coach access, was selected along the north fork of the Virgin River. The decision still is appreciated eighty years later.

Three miles into the canyon, leafy trees against Zion Canyon's wall frame the lodge. A towering cottonwood now anchors the two-acre carpet of sloping lawn.

Carl Croft was born in Canyon Country, and began working for Utah Parks Company after college in 1948: "Sitting in front of the lodge on

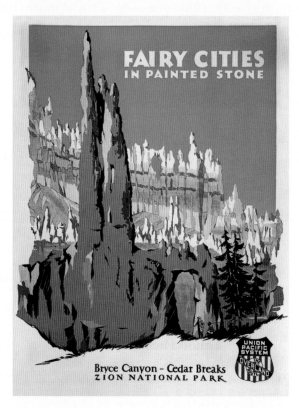

FAIRY CITIES
IN PAINTED STONE

Bryce Canyon - Cedar Breaks
ZION NATIONAL PARK

the beautiful lawn you are part of the canyon; it is part of you. You don't have to leave the lawn to see the canyon at Zion. You don't find that every place."

A railroad architect drafted the first lodge plans. Neither Mather nor Daniel Hull, landscape architect for the national parks, found the symmetrical design in keeping with the setting. Hull had another architect in mind for the job.

He suggested to his friend and colleague Gilbert Stanley Underwood that he apply for the job. According to Underwood's biographer, Joyce Zaitlin, Underwood was summoned to UP's Omaha headquarters to discuss the job in May of 1923. He was hired with little fanfare and sent to survey Zion and Bryce, where he did sketches. Here the young architect had an opportunity to apply principles from his Harvard education to the natural setting.

Underwood's first Zion Lodge drawing with a main lobby and spanning guestroom wings was rejected. Instead, Mather envisioned something less obtrusive. With the national parks on the brink of an influx of private car travel, Mather also wanted accommodations that would serve more than affluent rail travelers. Underwood's later attempts included the main lodge with surrounding Standard and Deluxe Cabins, a plan that was implemented in all of Underwood's work for the Utah Parks Company. Thus began a fruitful relationship between Underwood and both the Union Pacific and the National Park Service.

In 1924, a dining pavilion at Cedar Breaks and Zion Lodge opened. An extravagant celebration kicked off the 1925 season with government dignitaries and Union Pacific officials on hand to welcome visitors to Zion Park Lodge and the lodge at Bryce Canyon.

Additions and cabins were constructed on Zion and Bryce between 1926 and 1929. In 1928, Grand Canyon Lodge was completed on the North Rim of the Grand Canyon. Underwood was responsible for all of the work. With each plan, Underwood refined his approach to rustic architecture. He drew from the Arts and Crafts style that influenced the National Park Service, and developed elements that he would repeat throughout his career. Each successive stone and timber lodge became more dramatic while still reflecting its individual park.

"I think that Underwood was one of those cornerstones in the development of NPS rustic architecture. To build structures that are secondary to the landscape, something we should keep in mind today. To make sure these structures lie lightly on the land," observed Jack Burns who, as Zion's cultural resources specialist, oversees preservation issues for the NPS.

At Zion, the first floor of the two-story main lodge had a lobby and bathroom facilities, an office and store. The second level had a kitchen and dining room, and took advantage of the setting with a large balcony off the dining area.

Built of exposed frame construction, the balcony was supported by four large native sandstone columns reflecting the vertical lines of the park. Here was the beginning of the architect's making native stone the crux of his park designs. Centered behind the columns were full length, multi-paned windows on each level. Wood tongue and groove siding covered the exterior. A kidney-shaped swimming pool and two rustic bathhouses, designed by Underwood, were added later.

Built to last the length of UP's concession contract of twenty years, Zion Lodge weathered well. When Carl Croft began maintenance work at Zion twenty-some years after its opening, the 4x4 posts and tongue and groove on the inside were still in good shape.

Ten duplex Deluxe Cabins (1927) and five fourplex Deluxe Cabins (1929) randomly set along a pathway complemented the rustic design of the main lodge. Native stone fireplaces, chimneys and foundations, and exposed milled framing, gable roofs and front porches, were in keeping with NPS philosophy and the

When Zion Park Lodge opened, visitors were thrilled with the new facilities in Southern Utah, right, circa 1925, where they found suitable accommodations to use while touring the majestic park, below. The Union Pacific designed a plethora of advertising brochures often describing the region using storybook superlatives, facing page.

Map Showing Location of ZION GRAND CANYON BRYCE CANYON National Parks KAIBAB NATIONAL FOREST and CEDAR BREAKS

atmosphere of the park. The Deluxe Cabins also featured the luxury of hot and cold running water. Cabins were furnished with a day bed, a rollaway bed, rockers or armchairs, wicker writing desks and dressers with mirrors, wrought-iron lamps and tightly woven rugs. Simple standard cabins rounded out the guest accommodations.

Native sandstone was quarried within the park and at a site near Springdale during various stages of construction. Timber was another matter. At the turn of the 20th century David Flanigan had decided it would be much easier to cut timber on the rim above Zion and lower it to the canyon floor than to spend a week or two hauling it from the Kaibab Forest. After a few years of trial and error, he perfected a pulley system that made just such a plan reality. Flanigan purchased an existing sawmill and moved it to Stave Spring where the logs were milled before being lowered to the canyon floor, a trip of two-and-a-half minutes. The last major use of the cable system was in 1924, when it ferried lumber to build Zion Lodge.

Zion and the Canyon Country were ready to be "discovered" with the help of the Union Pacific's crack copy writers who created a marketing blitz promoting the "Colorful, Colossal, Sublime" sights with three-, four- or five-day Grand Circle tours.

Touring cars picked up rail passengers and were ready to roll. As the cars approached Zion, the sunroofs were peeled back, the women tied on their kerchiefs and everyone stared up at the wonders rising around them. Access to Zion was dramatically improved with the 1930 completion of the Zion–Mount Carmel Highway and mile-long tunnel that connected Zion more easily to Bryce and Grand Canyon national parks. With the improvements, visitorship skyrocketed from under 4,000 people in 1920 (prior to the lodge opening) to 55,000 in 1930 when facilities were in place along with a state-of-the-art road.

A visit to Zion, as with the other Canyon Coun-

try parks, was enhanced with ranger-led nature walks, horseback rides, campfire sing-a-longs and skits performed by summer employees, mostly students who worked double duty as maids, cooks, and bellmen. Visiting the Utah parks became a patriotic "Out West" experience. As with other national parks, one of the most loved traditions was the "sing-a-way" wherein employees gathered to greet and say goodbye to guests. Groups of visitors, the women usually dressed in billowing skirts and pearls, and men in natty casual attire, waved goodbye as they motored away.

It's not difficult to find someone who recalls past days at Zion National Park. There is a passion that draws each generation back. Judi Rozelle works as the NPS concession management analyst at Zion. "My grandfather Walter Ruesch was the first acting superintendent in 1919. My grandparents lived in the park before it was the park," she recalled. "My mother was assistant head housekeeper in 1949. I learned to swim at the old pool that used to be in front of the lodge. I took naps on the linen shelves and ate in the employee dining room. I have such a strong attachment; I was only four years old and I can remember walking on the path behind the old lodge."

Memories of the historic Zion Lodge now are just that. On January 28, 1966, the lodge burned.

"I was at the office in Cedar City. I got a call," recalled Carl Croft, then manager of facility maintenance for the UPC. "My crew burned it down. It was an accident—doing some repair work. A remodeling project where we were putting in new flooring and getting the old vinyl floor covering up.

"The railroad crew fought the fire as best they could until the park service got there with their pumper and their crew and knocked it

down in pretty fair order."

All that was left was the stone fireplace, pillars, and some of the kitchen equipment.

Executives at the railroad's Omaha headquarters decided to rebuild. "They had their own architect and in a few days they had preliminary drawings and in a couple of weeks they had the conceptual drawings," said Croft. "A couple of weeks later eight to ten truck loads rolled up, and in one hundred and eight days it was up and we were ready for business."

What had been built in those 108 days was a simple two-story utilitarian building with little appeal and none of the design and planning that went into earlier park architecture. "It was hideous," summed up Judi Rozelle. In 1992 a reconstruction effort added some of the original lodge's appearance to the new building, and included stone pillars and an expansive dining deck. On the inside the black and purple décor was replaced with knotty pine walls and enlarged historic photographs that tell the story of the lodge and park.

"It was very unfortunate that it burned down. When you go into national parks like at The Ahwahnee and Old Faithful you are in a 'lodge.' This one doesn't speak to it in the same way," said Jack Burns.

The Union Pacific promoted "Loop Tours" of southern Utah and North Rim of the Grand Canyon parks where they shuttled tourists who arrived via train at Cedar Breaks, Utah, facing page. Construction of the Zion-Mount Carmel Highway and Tunnel was an engineering feat that took hours off the drive, above. The UP's lodge at Zion burned in 1966, top, and was rebuilt in 108 days.

In 1992, reconstruction of the main lodge brought back some of the building's original appearance such as the stone columns, below, and the dining room deck from which guests can view Castle Dome, near left. Grounds include the giant cottonwood tree, from which visitors are treated to the splendid canyon scene, far left.

The historic Zion Lodge was lost, but the park's beauty is enhanced with noteworthy historic structures. In addition to the Deluxe Cabins, Underwood also designed the Women's Dormitory (1927); Zion Cafeteria/Inn (1934), now the Nature Center; the Men's Dormitory (1937); the Bake Shop (1931) later moved next to the Men's Dormitory and now used for storage; and a Mattress Shed moved from Birch Creek next to the Men's Dormitory.

From 1926 through 1928, Underwood turned his attention to constructing utility buildings in the Birch Creek Area that included the Horse Barn, Machine Shop, and Auto/Bus Storage Sheds.

"There's such a direct link to the [original] lodge and Birch Creek buildings. They were built by the UP and designed by Underwood. What's neat was Underwood's approach to a utilitarian building and his choice of materials," explained Jack Burns of the simple frame structures.

Over the years, the various cabins were updated and modernized. During the 1970s and into the 1980s, many of these historic structures, including the Underwood-designed Deluxe Cabins and dormitories, were in jeopardy of being removed. In 1976 the swimming pool and Underwood's bath houses were dismantled, and in 1984 the Standard Cabins were auctioned off and can be seen scattered around the state serving as summer cabins or storage sheds.

"The parks are great, but it's these buildings that show what man can do. I love these old buildings," said Carl Croft. "People too often forget about the buildings and the story never gets told."

In 1997 a historic structures report was filed and preservation plans outlined for the concessionaire, TWRS Recreational Services, and the

In 1997, the original Deluxe Cabins were restored. The majority of the work was on the interiors; the rough-cut stone and wood exteriors remain as Underwood designed them.

National Park Service. Since then, the Deluxe, now called Western, Cabins have been restored in keeping with their historic ambiance. The acoustic paneled ceilings were removed, exposing the rafters and vaulted ceilings and giving the cabins their original dimensions. Pressed board paneling was also removed, the chair railings returned, and the walls repainted to the original ivory tone. The exteriors had remained very much as Underwood had designed them. "The theme of those buildings, what you see on the outside, needs to be carried through to the interior. I think overall it was successful," said

Jack Burns of the project.

From April into October, visitors to Zion Canyon now see the park on foot or by shuttle bus. They have an opportunity to enjoy the canyon as early visitors once did. Around the lodge, they can loll on the lawn, walk along pathways between the historic cabins and buildings, play board games in the lobby, or sit on the lodge balcony.

"I can take the same old walks behind the lodge today," said Judi Rozelle as she recalled her childhood. "And I get that same old feeling."

Great White Throne and Red Arch Mountain, above, can be seen from Angels Landing, while plants like the flowering cactus, facing page, create the detail.

ZION NATIONAL PARK

RED, WHITE AND GREEN

"I was so impressed by the red cliffs and wilderness surroundings of Zion Canyon," wrote acting NPS superintendent Horace Albright of his 1917 visit, "that I determined we should expand Mukuntuweap (national monument) and have it made a national park. In some ways it was like a smaller and more colorful Yosemite. It had been described as "Yosemite painted in oils'."

What Albright saw in those red cliffs and layers of sedimentary rock was a stunning natural phenomenon dating back 250 million years. Albright hiked through the Narrows along the Virgin River and was up early the next morning to see "the sunlight creep down from the top of the domes and spires to the valley floor." The loveliness of the valley and beauty of the canyon walls overwhelmed him. Two years later, Zion became a national park.

Today the 229 square miles of Zion remain overwhelming. You can still hike the Narrows along the Virgin River that enters the park to the south and has carved a 2,000-feet deep chasm into the Markagun Plateau. The 12.5-mile trail is unmarked, and at some points the river is the trail. Most visitors prefer the Riverside Walk, among them is Tom Haraden, NPS assistant chief of interpretation. "I love rivers, so I love to walk the Riverside Walk. It used to be called Gateway to the Narrows now considered a backcountry experience. Here you get a sense of the Narrows by taking the Riverside Walk that is accessible to virtually everyone."

Dozens of other trails from an easy ten-minute stroll to two-day backpacking trips wind through the sandstone corridors. Perennial waterfalls drop into Emerald Pool, and the quarter-mile-long Weeping Rock trail takes you under a dripping wall of water.

A majority of the park's 2.5 million visitors follow the Scenic Drive through Zion Canyon

that passes formations such as The Grotto, The Great White Throne, The Organ, Weeping Rock ending at Temple of Sinawava. If you catch a spiritual tone here, it's for good reason. Zion is of another world.

"Most people are just in absolute awe that something this gorgeous exists," explained Judi Rozelle, who was born in the area and works for the National Park Service. "It's almost like a spiritual place. A place of calm and peace."

That sense of calm and peace has been recaptured in Zion Canyon with the opening of a transportation system for the 2000 season. From April through October private cars no longer clog the Scenic Drive. The park service suggests that visitors park in the town of Springdale and catch the shuttle at one of seven stops. They can walk across the footbridge at the park entrance and use the Visitor Center to plan their trip. At the other end of the plaza is the park shuttle. Hop on and you're off on the six-mile ride. There are eight stops with viewpoints and trailheads at each, and you can take time to trek or simply absorb the divine scope of the scenery.

The shuttle system has been a "huge success" and harkens back to the early park experience. "People used shuttles to begin with, and we use shuttles now; there was this little place in the middle where we used private cars," pointed out Tom Haraden.

While nature's handiwork is difficult to match, one engineering feat is worth observing. The Zion-Mount Carmel Highway and tunnel is a marvel. When it opened in 1930 visitors from Grand Canyon and Bryce Canyon national parks had easy access into Zion through the East Entrance.

In the far northwestern reaches of the park, you'll discover the Kolob Canyons off Interstate 15. Make sure to drive to the end of the road

where a stupendous view opens up that is totally hidden from the millions of cars that cruise by on the interstate. Kolob Arch, possibly the world's largest arch with a span of 310 feet, is a seven-mile hike from the Kolob Visitor's Center.

The climate ranges from arid desert to lush vegetation with ponderosa pine and spruce forests at the higher elevations that reach 7,000 feet. Cottonwood trees line the river bank caressing the canyon with rich green in the summer and a golden shimmer in the fall. Zion is blessed with the richest diversity of plants in Utah, almost 800 native species.

Seventy five species of mammals roam the park; the most commonly seen are mule deer and squirrels. Rare or endangered birds including peregrine falcons, Mexican spotted owls, willow fly catchers call the park home, but the most unique species in the park is one you can barely see. The Zion snail is the size of a pencil point. "What we have found is that the snail that is here has evolved so it has a larger foot than most snails for gripping," explained Tom Haraden. The Virgin River is definitely gripping territory. It may be short at 150 miles, but it is the steepest river in North American.

Zion park is open year round, but it is the late summer that Tom Haraden finds achingly beautiful. When the moisture has been sucked from the atmosphere leaving the sky a brilliant blue, he sees the perfect juxtaposition of color: "Cloudless dry deep-blue sky behind red cliffs behind these green green trees. I think that alone is something you won't see anywhere else."

A yucca blooms with Cable Mountain in the background, left. It was from the top of this mountain that a cable was rigged to lower timber for construction of Zion Park Lodge. Hikes, like that along Emerald Pool Trail, offer views in lush contrast to the limestone formations, below.

Architect Gilbert Stanley Underwood began Bryce Canyon Lodge as a simple design, facing page, later adding stonework and a gift shop and barbershop to the south end of the lodge, above.

BRYCE CANYON LODGE

OPENED 1925

The histories of the lodges at Bryce Canyon and Zion national parks are as interconnected as the wonders that first drew the curious to southern Utah. Both parks are part of a geologic formation called the Grand Staircase, gigantic steps of eroded cliffs of the High Plateaus whose varied bands of color highlight different formations as they descend toward the Grand Canyon. Both landscapes have been preserved and protected as national parks. Both of the parks' original lodges and surrounding cabins are the work of one architect, Gilbert Stanley Underwood, their ambitious development executed by one railroad, the Union Pacific (UP).

Yet each park and each lodge is like a sibling of the same parents who has developed its own features and personality.

The spectacle of Bryce Canyon unfolds from the rim, a panorama of pink, purple, orange,

and white limestone figures creating visions of oversized gargoyles, spires, temples, and arches set in gigantic scoops that span miles and drop 1,000 feet below. Bryce Canyon Lodge sits one-eighth mile from the plateau rim. The lodge setting at Zion rests three miles inside the canyon. At Bryce you look down and at Zion you gaze up.

Early native people inhabited the Colorado Plateau region for about 12,000 years, and Spanish explorers crossed the northwestern plateau of Arizona and to the southwest of Bryce Canyon in the late 1700s. Paiute Indians were living throughout the area when geological expeditions began surveying in the 1870s. As with Zion, early Mormon settlers explored the area in search of farmland, and established a sprinkling of settlements. Ebenezer Bryce came to the Paria Valley in 1875, and his neighbors

called the canyon behind his home Bryce's Canyon.

With its remote location and unfavorable growing climate Bryce Canyon was ignored for decades. That was to change.

J.W. Humphrey, U.S. Forest Service supervisor for the region, reluctantly visited Bryce Canyon in 1915. That reluctance morphed into enthusiasm, and he made it a personal campaign to open the area to the public. Humphrey hired photographers and brought the startling beauty of the region to the attention of the railroad companies. In 1918, the first newspaper account of the wonders of Bryce Canyon ran in the Sunday *Salt Lake Tribune.* The article, "Utah's New Wonderland," was the bench mark of southern Utah's tourist trade, and its title became one of UP's promotional slogans.

Two years earlier, Ruby and Minnie Syrett had decided to homestead near Bryce Canyon at a site a few miles from what is now Sunset Point. After the publication of "Utah's New

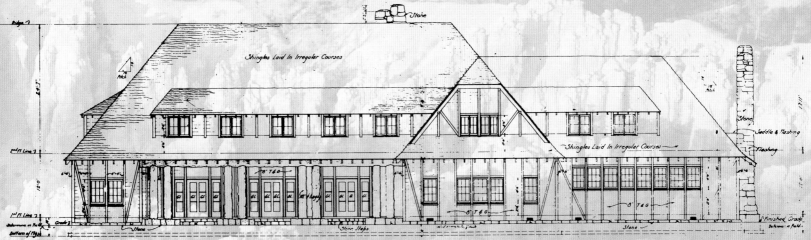

The Union Pacific's decision to use local timber and stone rather than shipping timber from the Pacific Northwest not only kept the cost down, but also assured that the building would fit with its setting, as seen here in 1937.

Wonderland," tourists began arriving to witness the exquisitely eroded amphitheater sculpted through the southern Utah landscape. The Syretts responded by pitching tents and preparing meals for the first visitors. They built Tourist's Rest, a rough-sawn log building and cabins, on the future site of Bryce Canyon Lodge. Eventually, the UP bought them out for $10,000.

While early railroad hotels had been built prior to the formation of the National Park Service in 1916, by the time development began at Zion and Bryce, the park service and its director, Stephen T. Mather, closely supervised them. Mather was not entirely enthusiastic about the Utah parks, in part because of the agency's small budget and staff. Once he committed to

overseeing the Zion National Park project, he set high standards and a tough approval process for structures at Zion, Bryce and, later, on the North Rim of the Grand Canyon.

Los Angeles architect Gilbert Stanley Underwood, who had been selected to tackle the Zion project, stopped at Bryce in 1923. He and others in the party selected the site knowing that building on the rim was not an option. The lodge site at Bryce Canyon was clearly less spectacular than Zion, but the lodge complex would evolve into an intimate example of rustic design that created a strong sense of place. Set at the edge of a small grove of ponderosa pines on the Paunsagunt Plateau, the lodge was within walking distance of the rim. Visitors had no idea of the view that awaited them as they stepped to

the observation area on its lip.

The UP purchased a portion of the site from the state and leased additional land from the U.S. Forest Service. Then, under pressure from Mather, in March of 1923, the UP spun off its subsidiary Utah Parks Company (UPC) to develop and operate the railroad's "Loop Tour" resort operations that would include Cedar Breaks, Zion, Bryce, and the North Rim of Grand Canyon, with a stop at Kaibab National Forest.

All the while, Utah Senator Reed Smoot was introducing various bills to protect the area. Bryce Canyon became a national monument in 1923. In 1927, UPC deeded its land to the federal government in return for a concession agreement and road improvements, opening the way for Bryce Canyon to become a national park on February 25, 1928.

During the progression to park status, work continued at the lodge site. UPC decided to use local timber and stone for construction. Rather than bring massive logs by rail from the Northwest, as had been done at El Tovar on the South Rim of the Grand Canyon, the lodge and cabins were constructed of local material—small milled lumber, and logs. Not only did UPC officials save money, but hiring local laborers also helped guarantee community support. The UPC signed a contract in the spring of 1923 with Ruby Syrett and Owen Orton to harvest timber.

Stone was quarried about one-and-a-half miles from the site. The railway wanted stone walls built "up to the snow line," feeling the timber was of "inferior quality," but Underwood's March 1924 elevation drawings indicate only stone foundation, chimneys, and steps. In fact, the steps were built with brick and most of the stone facade that now defines the lodge was added later.

It's likely that the lodge was meant as a temporary structure, to be used until the UPC could get permission to build on the edge of the rim. That would explain the simplicity of the original exposed-frame structure. Pairs of twenty-inch log columns supporting the portico along the front of the lodge, and a sweeping, wood-shingled, gable roof with shed dormer windows were the only exceptional details of the exterior. Underwood's plans called for shingles to be "laid in irregular course," a design that has continued with each new roof.

Jeff Stock, the parks historic preservation specialist, looks at the undulating shingle pattern as a craftsman's trademark. The great grandson of an early settler in nearby Canonville, he is familiar with the people of the region. "It was kind of a thing in the early 1900s where crafts-

Hickory tables and chairs filled the lobby where guests gathered around the radio after a day of hiking and riding, right. In 1988, work began on the restoration of the lodge that included recreating the lobby's original log light fixtures, below.

129

men wanted to leave their mark. A lot of the workers had one thing that was unique to them. That was their trademark. I think that played a part in the way the shingles were laid."

Reroofing using the original pattern is a slow process, but to Jeff Stock, that is part of his job: "The little things like that are what keep the integrity of the building."

The original portion of the lodge, finished for the 1925 summer season, included a lobby with information desk, post office, kitchen, and dining room, with guestrooms above the lobby and dining rooms. Bath facilities were on both floors.

Inside, a beautiful hammered-copper hood over the roughly-quarried stone fireplace in the lobby, and log and incandescent light bulb chandeliers gave the room—filled with hickory furniture—the requisite "lodge" feel.

In 1925, the Union Pacific began its advertising campaign: "America's Most Enchanting Vacation Land—Now Open. Here in Southern Utah are canyons preserving the flaming sunsets of a million years! Mountains of vermilion! Vast amphitheatres of filigreed stone stained with uncounted colors and studded with jewelled statues! Cathedrals, castles, pyramids, temples! Nowhere else are scenes so marvelous as in Zion National Park, Bryce Canyon–Cedar Breaks."

The first tourist season was a success beyond UPC President Carl R. Gray's expectations. In October 1925, he outlined a request to the Union Pacific in Omaha to build additional tourist facilities at both Zion and Bryce that would nearly double the lodge facilities. "In this season of three months we handled an aggregate of 1,847 rail passengers, and I am informed that this is a larger number than was handled by rail

the first year after the line was opened to West Yellowstone, and we have occasion to feel that is an auspicious beginning," Gray noted the following month in a proposal to Omaha.

If the lodge was meant to be temporary, plans to build another on the rim never materialized. Underwood began a series of expansion plans, and Bryce Canyon Lodge was transformed. In 1927, a gift shop, soda fountain, and barbershop were added on the south end of the building and the front portico extended along the addition. The following year, an auditorium was added to the southwest. Both rooms featured open ceilings with scissors trusses, horizontal wood paneling, and wood floors. A huge stone

fireplace occupies the south wall of the auditorium, and a panel of nearly floor-to-ceiling windows still fills the west wall. The dining room and kitchen were doubled in size, a basement was added under the kitchen expansion, and bath facilities were expanded. The wings not only added much-needed space, but also created a center courtyard. Outside, large cornerstone piers gave not only rustic detail but also a feeling of substance to the structure. A final touch, a sign with letters made of branches, "Bryce Canyon Lodge," still hangs today.

Next to the lodge, a complex of sixty-seven wood-frame standard and economy cabins housed guests and, by 1929, fifteen Deluxe Cabins were finished. The ten duplex and five quadruplex Deluxe Cabins reflect the rustic design the architect was fine-tuning, each featuring a steeply pitched gable roof, stone foundation and chimney, log-framed porches, and half-log-slab exterior walls.

Of all Underwood's UPC work, Bryce Canyon Lodge and Deluxe Cabins is the only project that remains intact. Grand Canyon Lodge burned in 1932, Zion Park Lodge burned in 1966, and the pavilion at Cedar Breaks is gone. Grand Canyon Lodge was rebuilt in 1937 using the remaining stone foundation; Zion Lodge was rebuilt on the original footprint, and has been updated. At Bryce Canyon visitors can enjoy an "Underwood" experience. While some of his Standard Cabins and most of the Housekeeping Cabins were removed, the Bryce Inn, now used as a camp store, is also an Underwood design, where recent restoration efforts have brought

BRYCE CANYON NATIONAL PARK

PRETTY IN PINK

There are moments in Bryce Canyon when you simply have to stop and thank your lucky stars that you've found this 52.6-square-mile splash of color in southern Utah. Below you is one amphitheater after another filled with spires, domes, arches, fins, pinnacles, and mazes—each tinted in the rich tones of red, yellow, and white too numerous to count. The development of the most stunning portions of this particular wonderland began about 60 million years ago and continues today.

After the sedimentation, compression, and uplift—and invading and receding waterways—had left the massive plateau, the relentless work of snowmelt and rain did much of the finish work. Streams cut away at the soft Claron limestone, sandstone, and mudstone, leaving the amphitheaters of Bryce Canyon and a dazzling gallery of sculpture.

This erosion helped shape the distinctive formations collectively referred to as "hoodoos" arranged in the horseshoe-shaped amphitheaters that scallop the eastern edge of the Paunsagunt Plateau. An early surveyor, Capt. Clarence E. Dutton, decided that this cavalcade of color created by various forms of iron oxide would be called the Pink Cliffs.

It is a pink you'll see nowhere else.

Everything outside of the canyon formations appears somehow less significant. Three overlapping vegetation zones sustain varied plant life. Sagebrush, juniper and piñon pine fill the lower elevations followed by ponderosa pine. The higher landscape is filled with white pine, white fir, blue spruce, aspen and bristlecone pine, one of the world's oldest known living things. Wildflowers bloom late in the high elevations, and six families of butterflies fill the park.

Coyotes, mountain lions, gray foxes, pronghorn (often called antelope), and a few black bears live in the park, but it is the mule deer, prairie dog, and chipmunk that you will become most familiar with. Hawks, woodpeckers, owls, stellar jays, and ravens are among the birds that fill the forest and the sky.

Hiking trails tailored to every level of exertion wind through the park. The Under Rim Trail extends twenty-three miles from Bryce Point to Rainbow Point with backcountry campsites along the way. The Rim Trail is a five-and-half-mile hike that takes you from Fairyland to Bryce Point. Even if you can't hike into this limestone Garden of Eden, viewpoints like Inspiration, Sunset, Sunrise, Bryce, and Fairyland Points are awe-inspiring.

For the 2000 season, Bryce instituted an optional-use shuttle system whereby you can leave your car outside the park and board buses that take you in. From the Visitor Center, three different "lines" take you to the famous viewpoints and trailheads, or on a more-limited-capacity tour of the park's southern portion.

James Woolsey, interpretive branch manager, sees it as an ideal way for hikers to approach the park. "You can take the shuttle to one place, go on a hike, then catch the shuttle to the next. The shuttle runs regularly through the entire park."

A perfect Bryce experience begins with sunrise. "All of the scenery is on the east side of the plateau, so this is much more of a sunrise than a sunset park," explained interpretive ranger Jan Stock. "Get out there at seven in the morning; that's the time to really see Bryce."

On an average day you can see landmarks that are 150 miles away.

Day hiking, interpretive ranger talks, or horseback riding fill the days, but don't forget the nights. With the clean, clear air, and distance from any city lights, the skies burst with stars, and there's nothing to compare to standing at Inspiration Point and counting shooting stars.

Sunset ignites the Amphitheater as seen from Bryce Point, facing page. Seemingly against nature, a pine grows amidst the hoodoos, above.

"Our night skies are unparalleled," added Stock.

Zion and Bryce and Grand Canyon national parks share an interrelated geologic history. As Woolsey explained, "From a geologic standpoint. Bryce is the youngest, Zion the middle aged and the Grand Canyon is the oldest. They tell the history of this portion of the earth."

It is a lavishly illustrated history sculpted and painted and preserved as one of this country's treasures.

Grand Canyon Lodge rises from the edge of the rim, above, but the original building, designed by Gilbert Stanley Underwood and burned in 1936, extended the canyon connection to the top of its watchtower, facing page.

GRAND CANYON LODGE

OPENED 1928

The current Grand Canyon Lodge, constructed in 1936 on the footprint of the original building, is a stunning structure. Its grand spaces open onto a panorama you can almost touch. Perched on the North Rim, it is as remarkable as it is inviting. But not as remarkable as the first limestone and wood structure designed by Gilbert Stanley Underwood. Here, on the less accessible side of the Grand Canyon, on the edge of Bright Angel Point, he created a precarious architectural wonder.

The Utah Parks Company (UPC) and National Park Service (NPS) were pleased with Underwood's work at Bryce and Zion national parks. They felt he could achieve equal success at their North Rim destination that would complete the Union Pacific railroad's plan for a "Loop Tour." UPC had purchased the Wylie tent camps on the North Rim in 1927 along with the transportation contracts, and it was ready to replace the spartan accommodations with a lodge and cabin complex.

Underwood was commissioned for the North Rim lodge on the heels of the completion of The Ahwahnee hotel in Yosemite National Park. Grand Canyon Lodge is architecturally and geographically linked to Bryce and Zion park lodges, but its elegance and panache seem to have sprung from the same inspiration that created the hotel in Yosemite. While The Ahwahnee's success had been the elegant incorporation of the

hotel with the towering walls of granite, on the North Rim the architect would look down for his inspiration. This was an unprecedented opportunity to create a lodge that drew from the architect's other work while incorporating a Southwestern theme. The National Park Service mandated that park buildings should be in keeping with their settings. Grand Canyon Lodge seemed an extension of that setting, a part of the geologic history that cracked and eroded the canyon wall.

The plan was for a U-shaped building that would welcome visitors arriving from the north, delivering them along a circle drive and all the while shielding the canyon view. From the lobby guests could see the dining room entrance to their right through a draped log-framed opening.

The registration desk was to the left with the recreation room behind that. But what drew them was the light.

"The original entrance of the lodge had this huge front of stone that went up, and it was really impressive to drive up there and get out of the coaches. That was part of it, to impress people—and to fool them. Inside you see the timber and stone work. You see the light, and that would draw people to the stairway, then into the sunroom," explained NPS interpreter Tom Carter. "You walked into the lobby, you followed the light and then BOOM! There's the Grand Canyon. Underwood did a trick here, a perception trick. I don't know where he got the idea. But that was genius."

Perched on the edge of the rim looking through floor-to-ceiling plate glass windows, visitors could feel a sense of vertigo as they pressed toward the windows.

Outdoor terraces and stairways cascaded from the building, and a watchtower protruded above. The rusticity was reinforced with wrought iron light fixtures, peeled log railings, and projecting log-ends. Low-pitched shingle or flat roofs, and horizontal siding, gave the building a sprawling appearance.

The main lodge's upper levels housed dormitory rooms and quarters for the lodge manager. A curio shop, kitchen, bakery, men's and women's toilet facilities (for

Standard Cabin guests) and storage areas filled the side wings of the U floor plan.

The same extensive use of stone and wood found on the exterior was carried to the inside. The dining room opened to expansive views with Underwood's favored scissors truss open-ceiling design used at The Ahwahnee and the auditorium at Bryce Canyon.

Along with the lodge, a series of cabins that filled NPS Director Stephen Mather's mandate for accommodations to meet most Americans' budgets. The Deluxe Cabins, a few with views as grand as those from the lodge, were wood frame with half-log siding situated on stone corner piers and stone foundations. The siding was chinked with cement and the textured limestone was laid with the rough side exposed. Gable roofs with wood shingles all featured peeled log entrances and porches on stone foundations that matched the chimneys and other stone work. Inside, stone fireplaces, exposed log ridgepoles and rafters and private bathrooms, and furnishings specifically placed in the architect's plans, created a sense of rustic elegance. The Standard Cabins were built of logs, with two units to each structure. Unlike the Deluxe Cabins, they were set more closely together. When completed in 1928, the complex consisted of the main lodge, one hundred Standard Cabins, and twenty Deluxe Cabins. In 1931, less-expensive Housekeeping Cabins were added near the campground with their own cafeteria and store for budget travelers.

Construction obstacles were as dramatic as the setting. Two hundred miles from the rail line with high altitude weather a problem, food and supplies were stockpiled so work could continue through the winter of 1927-1928. About 125 men worked at the construction site, and fifteen brought their families. A stonemason's wife was a teacher and took it upon herself to set up a

The lodge construction offered a sight for workers, left. A fireplace was built in the sunroom, but the draw of the space was the wall of windows, below.

school and instruct the children—without pay.

Unlike The Ahwahnee, with its design and construction problems, this building rose in record time. Timber was harvested from the Kaibab Forest and processed at a sawmill moved to the site. A limestone rock quarry was opened two miles from the site, and a handful of talented stonemasons from southern Utah towns did the rockwork. According to Underwood biographer Joyce Zaitlin, UP officials "considered the use of steel or concrete too costly for such a remote area," so the framing and exterior, if not stone, was wood.

The site had no source of water, so a hydroelectric plant was constructed at Roaring Springs 3,400 feet below the rim. That construction was possible by using a cable tram that carried construction material from the rim over the sheer cliffs to the hydroelectric plant site in the "hole" below. George Croft was hired to manage the power plant, and that was where his son, Carl, spent the summer of 1928 with his parents and two siblings.

High above them, on June 1, 1928, the lodge and cabins opened with accommodations for 250 guests. "It harmonizes perfectly with its sublime surroundings and seems itself a work of nature," read one UP brochure. But there was more than advertising hype. The park superintendent wrote in his annual report that the lodge's completion was "one of the most important steps in the history of the Park."

The architect was in his prime, and the Grand Canyon Lodge design drew from his other national park work, particularly The Ahwahnee. While not meant to be as luxurious as The Ahwahnee, it was as successful. Underwood was no doubt influenced by another architect, Mary Colter, whose 1914 buildings (Lookout Studio and Hermits Rest on the South Rim of the canyon) seem to be

In 1930, employees gathered in front of the lodge to welcome guests, below. On September 1, 1932, disaster struck when the structure was destroyed by fire, leaving nothing but smoldering ruins.

The lodge was rebuilt on the original stone foundation, and diners are served up incomparable views with their entrees, above. As with the original design, the lodge obstructs the view and visitors' first sight of the canyon is after going through the entry and lobby then into the sunroom, facing page.

natural extensions of the landscape. While smaller in scale and without Underwood's elegant detail, their sites, Southwestern influence and use of blocks of native rock and timber may have inspired Underwood.

"I have a feeling that he was trying to match what had been done on the South Rim. I think at that point, he wanted to match it because Mary Colter had done such great work on the other side. I really feel, and I have no proof, that he was aware of her work," suggested Tom Carter. "And he learned a lot at The Ahwahnee that was translated to the North Rim lodge."

With the lodge's completion, the Union Pacific's grand "Loop Tour" was a reality. Not only were the lodges and cabins in place, but the Utah Parks Company also had purchased transportation contracts between Cedar City and Zion and constructed a tour-bus terminal in Cedar City where they had bought the Escalante Hotel. The most extensive of the Circle Tours was Grand Tour No. 5, which began from Cedar City where trains dropped off tourists at the "Gateway to the Parks," then took them by bus to Zion National Park, Kaibab Forest, the North Rim of the Grand Canyon, Bryce Canyon, and Cedar Breaks.

In 1930, a final link was added to the complex plan when the Zion–Mount Carmel Highway opened, an engineering feat and joint effort of the UPC, the NPS, the state of Utah, and the Federal Highway Administration. The highway and mile-long tunnel offered not only a more direct route between Zion, Bryce, and the North Rim, but also a thrilling ride.

Then, on September 1, 1932, disaster struck. Grand Canyon Lodge and two Deluxe Cabins burned in the largest structural fire in Grand Canyon's history. A telegram sent late in the day said that the fire had been discovered by a night porter "at approximately 3:50 a.m." Sirens were blown, fire alarms activated, employees evacuated

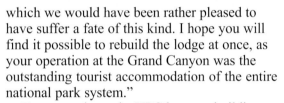

and workers began battling the blaze. After fighting the fire for "about seven minutes and apparently making headway, water pressure in the hose being used…decreased to extent that they with all others assisting could not retard further progress of the fire."

All that remained were stone walls, foundation, terraces, stairways and fireplaces. The UPC's decision to forgo building with steel would haunt them.

"Oh, it was smoldering for two days. I was at Grand Canyon Lodge the day after it burned down. It was still smoldering," recalled Carl Croft, who like his father would become supervisor of facility maintenance for UPC. "I was seven years old. It was all those big bleak stone columns just standing there. Then you realized all the wood was gone. Nothing but stone columns and ghosts were all there was: mostly charred black ghosts."

The fire devastated not only UP officials and a small boy, but also Horace Albright, then NPS director, who wrote:

"The news came to me as a great shock. It seemed a crime that this wonderful Lodge had to be destroyed when there were fully a score of old lodges, hotels, government structures, etc.

which we would have been rather pleased to have suffer a fate of this kind. I hope you will find it possible to rebuild the lodge at once, as your operation at the Grand Canyon was the outstanding tourist accommodation of the entire national park system."

Two years later, the UPC began rebuilding the lodge on the remaining stone foundation, but there is no evidence that Underwood took part in its design. It is likely that responsibility fell to a UP architect, perhaps W.H. Wellman, who drew the first rejected plans for Zion Park Lodge and was the UP architect in 1936. UPC directed the operation and hired Ryberg Brothers builders of Salt Lake City to salvage as much of the stone as possible in their reconstruction. The first floor plan remained much the same, although a tearoom was added and spaces reconfigured, particularly in the side wings.

The original recreation hall had a beamed flat ceiling and the new version features a pitched roof with a vaulted ceiling. Instead of log trusses in the lobby and recreation and dining rooms, steel beams covered by wood slabs to resemble peeled beams were used. Inside, Grand Canyon Lodge retains or perhaps has more drama than the original building. But the

marvelous sense of the building in perfect harmony with the rim was partially lost. From the canyon wall, the original lodge still rises, but the asymmetrical "stairstep quality" of the walls and rooflines with their rich texture are mostly gone. Instead, the design was simplified and capped with a traditional green gable roof.

The surviving Deluxe Cabins and the reconstructed lodge opened on June 1, 1937. That year, guests returned with the option of Deluxe Cabins for $6 a day for one person or $8.50 for two, with thrifty Housekeeping Cabins running $2.25 a day for one or two guests.

The Utah Parks Company continued to operate the "Loop Tour" facilities until 1972. Adapting through the years to the changing tastes of the touring public, UPC deeded the North Rim properties, along with their properties in Zion and Bryce, to the National Park Service. When the North Rim opens each May, visitors return to see the wonder of it all.

"In the new Visitor's Center they keep asking, 'Where is the Grand Canyon?' 'Go inside the lodge,' I tell them," Tom Carter explained of the summer refrain. "And POW! there it is. It's still the most incredible thing about that lodge."

GLACIER PARK

Glacier National Park and the Great Northern Railway
creations in and bordering the park are as interconnected
as rails at a switching station. In the majesty
of Montana's Rocky Mountains are historic alpine hotels
and chalets connected by trail, boat, and road systems
that remain as links to the past.

Flower gardens line the path to Glacier Park Lodge, above, where visitors were once greeted by members of the Blackfeet tribe, facing page, as they arrived.

Trains still stop at Glacier Park Station as they did in 1913. Today, most visitors arrive by car or tour bus, but those who take the *Empire Builder* share an experience much like that of early visitors to Glacier Park Lodge. What train passengers found after their journey west across the Great Plains was a buffer between the expansive yawn of the plains and the jagged teeth of the Rocky Mountains.

"It's basically the same today," explained Dan Engstrom, project line supervisor on the *Empire Builder.* "For hours you are going across these vast plains—an endless sea of land. Then between five and six o'clock, the mountains loom before you like a huge wall. In my experience, there is a silent stare. People are in awe. Watching them is like watching your kids open presents at Christmas."

Early guests stepped off the train, and "unwrapped" before them was the panorama of the huge log lodge set against the mountain horizon. The manicured lawn was dotted with teepees, and the 1,000-foot garden path was banked with specially ordered flowers planted by the Swiss gardener.

Before encountering the "real" wilds of Glacier National Park, guests could decompress at a lodge big enough to be in keeping with its environment, yet as civilized as any eastern or European hotel.

In 1895, the U.S. government had acquired a ceded portion of the Blackfeet Reservation east of the Continental Divide for $1.5 million and promptly opened it for mining exploration. Ore

deposits proved minuscule, and serious lobbying began for national park status. In 1910, thanks in part to the efforts of James J. Hill, founder of the Great Northern Railway, and his son Louis, Congress finally passed and President William Howard Taft signed a bill creating Glacier National Park.

James J. Hill saw the Great Northern as predominantly a transcontinental freight line, but he and Louis advocated development—whether agricultural, mercantile or tourist—along its tracks. But it was Louis Hill who welcomed the potential in passenger travel—especially to Montana's Glacier country. Louis had put in his time with the Great Northern beginning after his 1893 graduation from Yale, and proved himself worthy of filling his father's

formidable shoes. He assumed the presidency of the railway in 1907.

In Montana, Louis saw not only an opportunity to offer tourists an alternative to Yellowstone National Park, served by the Northern Pacific Railway, or the Grand Canyon, on a spur of the Atchison, Topeka & Santa Fe Railway line, but also his chance to develop a project that was his own.

Louis Hill was so dedicated to promoting Glacier National Park and constructing his dream, that in December 1911 he temporarily stepped down as president of the Great Northern Railway to devote his time to these projects. "The work is so important that I am loath to intrust the development to anybody but myself," he explained to the press.

With few funds for park development, the first Glacier Park superintendent and his Washington, D.C., colleagues were eager to accept the railway's largess, and Louis Hill obliged. He combined business resources, marketing savvy, and political connections to pave the way for a construction project unequaled in any national park.

While Hill's initial foray into tourist facilities began at Belton on the west side of the park, his major development unfolded on the eastern side of the Continental Divide.

By 1912, Hill had secured a special Act of Congress giving the railroad the right to purchase 160 acres of land on the Blackfeet Indian Reservation just outside the park at

The depot timbers perfectly frame Glacier Park Lodge.

Midvale station (now Glacier Park Station). The station depot and Glacier Park Hotel (later changed to Lodge) would be followed by the Many Glacier Hotel, nine chalet "camps," the Prince of Wales Hotel in Glacier's sister park, Waterton Lakes National Park—along with miles of roads and trails, a telephone system, and trail ride, motor touring, and boat services.

Glacier Park Hotel would become the Great Northern's "Gateway to Glacier," and while Hill admired Swiss design, he wanted more than an alpine chalet for his signature hotel. Hill turned to the state of Oregon for inspiration. In 1905,

the Oregon Historical Society had sponsored the Lewis & Clark Exposition in Portland. Eleven states erected buildings, but the darling of the expo was the Oregon Forestry Building. Hill and his father were particularly taken with the structure, which was meant to promote Oregon wood products. Other expositions had featured huge log buildings, but none was quite as successful as the Forestry Building.

Massive forty-eight-foot-high logs formed the Forestry Building's colonnade. Skylights topped the pitched roof. In 1911, Hill had the plans, over thirty pictures, and the cost of the

structure sent to his architect, S.L. Bartlett. Hill's father had donated money to preserve and maintain the Forestry Building after the exposition, a donation mentioned in correspondence to acquire the plans. Bartlett had tracings made of the plans and returned them to Portland, as he noted in a memo to Hill in September 1911.

What Bartlett, with the assistance of Thomas McMahon, then created in Glacier Park Hotel was a chalet with dimensions that reflected America's West.

In addition, Hill masterminded a national advertising campaign that labeled Glacier

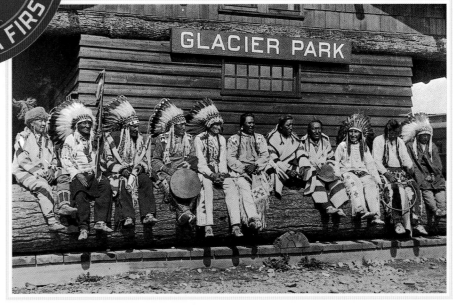

National Park as "America's Alps" and implored travelers to forgo Europe and "See America First." Everyone from presidents to journalists was entertained at the park. The *New York Times* "Annalist" wrote, "next to Col. Roosevelt, L.W. Hill is about the best advertising man in the United States." Hill hired artists, filmmakers, and photographers to capture the beauty of the region, and took the exhibit on a special train to bring the park to the people. On that train were members of the Blackfeet tribe who attended any public event the publicity department could muster up, as diverse as football games and operas. By 1914, the railway's Glacier advertising budget exceeded $300,000 a year.

During the summer season, Blackfeet in full ceremonial dress were hired to greet arriving passengers, put on evening programs, and work at jobs from chef to switchboard operators.

As a young man, Hill had camped and hunted in the area and made friends with the local Blackfeet. To Hill, hiring Blackfeet to work for him was not only good for the Great Northern, but also good for the Blackfeet. In 1912 Hill was adopted into the Blackfeet tribe and given the name of Gray Horse Rider.

Jack Gladstone, son of a Montana Blackfeet father and a German American mother, is co-founder of Native America Speaks lecture series meant to deepen the visitor's knowledge and appreciation of the Blackfeet's relationship with Glacier National Park. During that time when the social trend was to destroy the Indian culture, Gladstone believes that bastions like Glacier Park and Buffalo Bill's wild west show also were opportunities for Indians.

"Louis Hill was a friend. There are the critics who say the Indians were being exploited. Another way of looking at it," explained Gladstone, "is that Glacier represented a certain

The Great Northern Railway challenged citizens to "See America First." Blackfeet tribe members in full ceremonial garb were hired to greet rail passengers when they arrived at East Glacier, right. Today, the Empire Builder *brings guests to Glacier much as it did in 1913, below.*

Louis Hill celebrated the opening of Glacier Park Lodge on the 75th birthday of his father, James J. Hill, upper right, in the great hall that offers the same forest setting today, lower right. Louis was adopted into the Blackfeet tribe; pictured with Wades-in-the-Water in 1925, above.

economic opportunity to continue being who we were. Mildly exploitative, perhaps; however, Glacier did not damage us. If anything it was a time to look forward to in the summer, people would be happy again and there was work."

Along with the Blackfeet, formally attired drivers and bellmen in polished knee-high boots were on hand to escort guests to the gigantic rustic "chalet" with teepees set up on the lawn, through a Chinese pagoda festooned with cherry blossoms, and into the great hall. After experiencing this collage of cultures, visitors encountered their first woodland experience. It was indoors.

Guests stepped through the front door into a perfectly appointed "forest." Twenty-four forty-eight-foot-high, four-foot-wide Douglas-firs line the colonnade of the 200-by-100-foot soaring lobby that is flanked by galleries on either side. Tree bark remains on all of the fifteen- to eighteen-ton vertical timbers, with light filtering through three atrium windows that straddle the sixty-foot-high peak of the roof. Instead of green boughs, Ionic capitals top the massive log columns. Peeled cedar railings inset with St. Andrew's crosses rim the two staggered balconies.

While the image is rustic, the rectangular basilica design is derived from that of Roman halls, which was adopted as a building type for early Christian churches. The lobby is a sanctuary of sorts and reflects the idea of architecture as symbol, not just shelter. To Louis Hill, the symbol was based on European cathedrals, a place to praise both the beauties of the park and the free enterprise system that made the building possible.

When Hill's workers unloaded freight cars carrying more than sixty huge timbers, from thirty-six to forty inches in diameter, the astounded Blackfeet are said to have dubbed the new building "Oom-Coo-Mush-Taw" or "Big Trees Lodge." It's no wonder. Trees of that size didn't grow in Montana, and since Hill wanted the same impressive colonnade as the Forestry Building, he had the firs sent by rail from the Pacific Northwest. By April 1912 all of the oversized timbers were on their way to the site.

The Great Northern Railway had contracted with Evensta & Company, of Minneapolis, to construct the building, and by March, Bartlett and the contractor were staking out the hotel. Meanwhile, a spur track was being completed to transport the timber now waiting at Whitefish and Essex. Construction began in April, and fifteen months later, the hotel was completed.

The grand opening was held June 15, 1913, the seventy-fifth birthday of James J. Hill. Six hundred invitations went out to James Hill's friends and associates, including the railway's engineers, conductors, brakemen, and station agents. Following the luncheon celebration held in the hotel's great hall, each guest toured the park by auto or horseback, or on foot.

Louis Hill was a "hands on" manager. At Glacier he negotiated concession agreements and land deals with the government, planned a park-wide concept of chalets and hotels linked by trails, designed a transportation system that included hiking, horses, cars, buses, boats, and trains, and kept his thumb on construction costs—and he personally selected everything for the décor, from paper lanterns to a mounted eagle his son had shot.

"I want to have the eagle that Louis killed recently mounted. I want him in the Glacier Park Hotel lobby…I wish you would call up Mrs. Hill and get the eagle and have it mounted wherever you think best, instructing them to make a very wide spread of the wings and have the eagle in a flying position," he wrote while in Minot, North Dakota, on November 30, 1914.

Hill's taste seemed as eclectic as his duties. Indian pictographs still decorate the walls above huge picture windows in the lobby. Animal horns and skins, buffalo skulls (some reproduced in plaster of Paris), and teepees, Blackfeet crafts, rugs, blankets, and basketry filled the lobby. To emphasize the "camp" feel of the "forest lobby," as a railway brochure of the time described it, was a copper-hooded, open fireplace at one end and a more traditional stone fireplace at the other. While totem poles stood on the front porch, Japanese lanterns hung from the rafters inside.

The staff was part of the décor. Besides the Blackfeet Indians—whom Hill sometimes referred to as the "Glacier Park Tribe"—staff serving tea was dressed in kimonos, while others were outfitted in Bavarian uniforms.

"Years before Walt Disney, Hill created a theme park with multiple (and often culturally confused) themes that met multiple expectations," noted historian Ann Emmons. "American tourist dollars were kept at home and travelers' demands for a 'western' cultural experience, complete with Indians, and for physical comforts more-often associated with foreign travel, were simultaneously met."

"Hill had marketing panache. With 'See America First' he was competing with the tourists who would spend their summer in Europe. In terms of the architecture and design, he made changes to draw those tourists," added Barbara Pahl of the National Trust for Historic Preservation. "The whole thing is the unexpected—then you have this international hotel experience."

The international flavor also reflected the business interests of the Great Northern. The railway encouraged tourism to Seattle and Alaska, and its premier train was called the *Oriental Limited.* The Great Northern also

formed the Great Northern Steamship Company to trade with Japan. If the décor with its advertising undercurrent was too confusing, guests could simply walk out onto the expansive veranda running the length of the lodge and gaze at the imposing mountain range artistically composed without the help of man.

Today, the lanterns and most of the original lobby furniture and accessories are gone. An original half-log table and baby grand piano remain, and a mountain goat (the Great Northern's mascot) is mounted in the center of the lobby. Three oversized chandeliers with Mission style lanterns and matching sconces light the space. Portions of the hardwood floors are now carpeted. The open fireplace was removed after it caused more than a "camp" fire.

The cocktail lounge, once on the balcony, now fills half of the west lobby, with picture windows opening up the entire wall. At one time, the space served as the rest area for the Blackfeet between their evening shows. Outside, oversized hickory chairs fill the veranda on the west, and flowers still line the garden path at the entry.

Windsor-style chairs surround the tables in the dining room as they did in 1914. Wagon-wheel chandeliers have replaced at least two other vintages of light fixtures, including the original Japanese lanterns and the milk-glass globes of the 1940s. The original clinker brick fireplace, with hooks and a simmering shelf, anchors one wall.

The plunge pool in the basement was filled in and the space used for cabaret shows.

Almost as soon as the sixty-one-room hotel was completed, Hill ordered an expansion. A four-story annex, connected by a wide breeze-way, added 111 rooms to the hotel. The breeze-way created one of the most charming additions to the lodge, a departure from the huge, imposing great hall. The breezeway is banked on both sides by windows and topped with the timber beams and trusses of the open ceiling. Filled with Morris chairs, card tables and desks, it is used today as it was originally intended. Guests read, write letters, play cards or enjoy the scenery from a sunny, sheltered vantage point. By the time the annex was completed, Glacier Park Lodge cost $500,000 to construct and furnish.

Guestrooms were intended for the sophisticated traveler. Private baths, fireplaces, porches, and suites were all available. Each room was meticulously furnished, and original guestroom pieces remain. Glass shades were custom-ordered from Pittsburgh, and rooms were decorated with sturdy oak furniture, Navajo rugs, china candlesticks, and Hudson Bay blankets.

The exterior of both the main lodge and the annex features a pitched roofline with long shed dormers running nearly the entire length of the roof. Arched brace roofs extend over balconies in the annex (in much the same fashion as on the Forestry Building), supported by massive timbers, with jigsaw balustrades between board railings that add a Swiss touch. The main building has peeled log railings along the balconies and porches, and shingles between the gables. The plan called for log exterior on the main building, but that was changed to clapboard siding and shingles. The Great Northern hotels first were coated with a creosote stain, but now are painted "national park brown."

By the end of 1914, Glacier Park Hotel Company, a subsidiary of the Great Northern Railway, took over ownership and operation of the railway's hotels and camps in the park. The company gave Glacier Park Lodge a golf course, built in 1928, and an outdoor swimming pool.

The combination of the Great Depression and the switch in travel tastes of the American public

There is no shortage of views from the lodge whether guests are dining, facing page, or spending time in the breezeway, above.

from rail car to automobile dramatically changed visitor dynamics. The railroad's tie to the park began to unravel.

In 1946, the Great Northern initiated advertising to sell its Glacier properties. Finally, in 1960 Glacier Park, Inc., with Donald Hummel as president, purchased the hotels. Today, Glacier Park Lodge is owned and operated by Glacier Park, Inc., now a subsidiary of Viad Corp.

Glacier Park Lodge lacks the official recognition of a National Historic Landmark, yet it remains the Gateway to Glacier.

"The collections of buildings that are left in Glacier are precious and irreplaceable. We want to make sure these buildings are here to greet a whole new generation of visitors who come to the park—so they can have the experience that Louis Hill envisioned back in 1910 when the park was created," observed Barbara Pahl. "He had a fabulous vision of how to see it and experience it. We want to preserve the place and the experience."

Belton Chalet's Swiss design, as seen in watercolor renderings done by Cutter & Malgrem of Spokane, Washington, facing page, was brought back after extensive restoration. The chalet complex reopened and was named a National Historic Landmark in May 2000, above.

BELTON CHALET

OPENED 1910

Tucked against the hillside past the west entrance of Glacier National Park stands Belton Chalet. The chocolate brown cluster of perfectly restored buildings was the first foray of the Great Northern Railway and its president, Louis Hill, into tourist development in Glacier.

The Swiss chalet was completed in 1910, the same year that Glacier became a national park. Here rail travelers disembarked at the new depot on the fringe of vast wilderness, and walked under a pergola through landscaped grounds to an intimate Swiss chalet. Across the railroad tracks unfolded a hint of Glacier National Park.

Louis Hill's father, Great Northern founder James J. Hill, had completed his line over the Continental Divide via Marias Pass into northwestern Montana in 1891. The following year Great Northern (GN) set up a station that was soon named Belton. A boxcar served as a depot, and by 1900 the stopover had spawned homesteads, shops, and a post office around the station and along the shore of pristine Lake McDonald three miles away.

Outdoorsmen, conservationists, small-time entrepreneurs, homesteaders "living off the land," and the Great Northern all vied for a piece of the Glacier pie. The railway's agents sent explorers to assess tourist potential in the glacier-cut valleys and peaks beginning in 1894. On the east side of

the Continental Divide, the U.S. government acquired a ceded portion of the Blackfeet reservation for $1.5 million in 1895. On the west side of the divide, the Lewis and Clark Reserve was established in 1897 under the Forest Reserve Act, and included land around Belton Station.

Louis Hill was more than smitten with Montana's wild scenery. In 1909, while lobbying for passage of legislation to establish the national park, he described Lake McDonald as "one of the most beautiful bodies of water to be

found anywhere, ten and one-half miles long and three miles wide, in a valley surrounded on the east, west and south by virgin and unscarred forests extending up to the snow line, while the head of the lake presents a panorama of the most rugged, sharp mountain peaks."

In 1910, thanks in part to the efforts of Louis Hill and his father, Congress finally passed and President William Howard Taft signed a bill creating Glacier National Park.

With the park a reality, Louis Hill turned his considerable talent to developing park facilities for GN's passengers. His vision was for a cohesive European system of grand hotels, roads, and trails through the park, with a series of backcountry camps and chalets each a day's ride from the next. With his investment in passenger travel, he was not about to wait for the government to build proper facilities.

Hill's skills included an incredible eye for detail. He studied Swiss architecture, ordering European books on the subject. To transform his vision into reality, he turned to the Spokane architectural firm of Cutter and Malmgren for the first renderings for Belton Chalet. Kirtland Cutter had incorporated the idea of Swiss chalet design into western settings, and his drawings and the completed structure are strikingly similar.

GREAT NORTHERN RAILWAY'S GLACIER BENCHMARK
WEST GLACIER, MONTANA

The three-story chalet is the most overtly Swiss building in what would become Hill's Glacier country building spree. The gable roof with deep overhangs was topped with boards and stones in the Swiss tradition, and gracefully curved and cut corbels supported the beams. Built of milled lumber, log, rubble stone, and river rock, it was stained dark brown. Jigsawn balustrades surrounded the balconies, and windows featured leaded panes. Inside, ten guest chambers, a lobby, and a dining room were furnished in the popular Arts and Crafts style. A stone fireplace anchored the lobby, and fir wainscoting warmed its walls. Family-style meals were prepared from fruits and vegetables bought in Kalispell, Montana, fresh meat ordered from Spokane, Washington, and non-perishables shipped from St. Paul, Minnesota.

Guestrooms featured rustic rockers and brass or iron beds made up with white sheets, bed felts, quilts, and wool blankets. Simple "Swiss" curtains covered the paned windows.

"When people would get off the train—let's face it—this was first class in 1910," explained local historian Bob Jacobs, who leads interpretive tours of the Belton buildings.

In 1911, Belton's popularity prompted the construction of two cottages and an artist's studio with additional guestrooms. The cottages, now named Lewis and Clark, featured inviting front porches beneath overhanging eaves finished with jigsawn balustrades. Inside, brick fireplaces warmed the sitting room; three bedrooms and a bath completed each oasis.

"But after the Great Northern built the chalet they didn't know what to do with it," said Bob Jacobs, "so they put the operation under the Dining and Sleeping Car Department. They found that operating a land-based hotel was significantly different than running a rolling hostelry." Eventually, a separate company was formed to run all of the Great Northern's Glacier properties.

The chalet's manager was Fiametta Fery, daughter of John Fery, the artist who was under contract with the Great Northern to paint mountain scenes used in the railway's promotions. The Fery family moved from St. Paul to Glacier for the 1911 season, and it seems likely that the studio with skylights was used by Mr. Fery. Hill visited the chalet at the end of the season, and pointed out that the "object in putting Mr. Fery's family on this work was to interest Mr. Fery to make the Park his permanent home…You can readily see," he wrote, "the advantage of having a scenic artist permanently in the Park."

In 1912, Superintendent William Logan reported that Belton "met with universal satisfaction" of the "high-class travel" patrons who frequented the facility during a long summer season. For three winters beginning in 1911, Superintendent Logan used the chalet as park headquarters.

The original chalet was expanded and in 1913 a "dormitory" with twenty-four guestrooms and a large lobby was constructed behind the chalet and cottages. The long horizontal expanse of the dormitory, now restored

In 1913, passengers stepped off the train into Glacier country at Belton station, where a band greeted them.

as the "lodge," is broken with a jerkinhead gable and two levels of balconies. Around the buildings, Hill seemed particularly interested in creating gardens, arbors, and a lush lawn.

As the hotel and dining accommodations at Belton were completed, Louis Hill's focus turned from West Glacier to the east side of the park. What Belton's setting lacked in drama, it had made up for in convenience, but park guests were clamoring for more in destination resorts placed in spectacular settings. The lovely enclave at Belton had been a testing ground for Hill's grand vision. With the completion of the Great Northern's Glacier Park Station, Glacier Park Lodge, and the backcountry chalets and camps followed by Many Glacier Hotel, Belton was all but forgotten. It was eliminated from the GN's brochures, and during the 1920s maintenance slipped. In 1930, the kitchen and dining room were closed. The much ballyhooed Highway 2 opened in 1932, cutting between the chalet complex and the Belton Depot. During the winter of 1936, the depot was skidded to its present location about one quarter mile from the chalet, and expanded; it reopened in 1937.

The Great Northern divested itself of Belton Chalet and its surrounding buildings in 1946, and for decades the Luding family used portions of the complex as an office and storage space, and periodically operated a restaurant here.

The Belton Chalet complex that visitors see today is again that charming enclave of 1914. In 1997, Cas Still and her husband, Andy Baxter, bought the property and began a three-year restoration that would bring back the original grouping of a hotel, cottages, and restaurant. The process was meticulously done, and Belton Chalet, Lodge and Cottages were named a National Historic Landmark in May 2000 as part of the Great Northern Railway Historic Landmark District. (The studio still stands, but

When Belton Chalet opened in 1910, rail travelers disembarked at Belton station and walked to the Great Northern's first hotel in Glacier, top. The main chalet was expanded, and two cottages, a dormitory, and a studio (not seen) were constructed, above.

it is no longer part of the property.) Belton Chalet's renovation also received a special award from the National Trust for Historic Preservation.

Restoration of this magnitude by private owners seems overwhelming. At times it was.

"It was all a challenge," explained Cas Still as she walked through one perfect space after another. "It was huge. The scale and size. Something so immense took so much time and planning."

The first winter was the "dumpster" season as Still called it, when the couple and a local crew dug through debris, sorting the treasures from the trash. Then they evaluated the structural situation and, with a crew that included consulting, historical and landscape architects, contractors, builders, and an interior designer, they began. The original chalet's balconies and decks were long gone, and berms of dirt from the construction of Highway 2 pressed against the lower level. Digging, crawling, and jacking up the building were just the beginning. New balconies, now meeting accessibility requirements, grace the building, their balustrades reproduced to match the original design.

The basement was excavated and a kitchen created in what was once a dirt-floored cellar. The main floor houses the Dining Room, Tap Room, and Gift Shop. Just outside is a gigantic cylinder barbecue—the chalet's old boiler transformed by Andy Baxter—as part of an outdoor kitchen. Comfy chairs and settees surround the Tap Room fireplace, and simple Arts and Crafts décor fill both rooms. Walls are covered with wainscoting and plaster, and an original Fred Kiser photograph of Lake McDonald—discovered in a closet—hangs in the Dining Room.

Upstairs, guest chambers were reconfigured for staff housing and office space, and the upper reaches of the chalet now form a small staff apartment.

What was once a separate "dormitory" building holds the main lobby, twenty-five guestrooms with private baths, and a recreation room. The building had been boarded up for so long that the new owners were able to identify original paint colors, curtains, and furniture.

"Those were the clues. Basically we took what was here and then built things that looked like it and found similar styles," explained the proprietress, who credits the Luding family with preserving the property so "we could restore it."

The original piano is in the lobby that is also furnished with a combination of family treasures and original pieces. Tulip light fixtures hang in the hallways and in guestrooms where the original iron beds, rebuilt dressers, and rockers for the balconies appear. Simple coverlets drape beds made up with fresh ivory linens. Guests crawl into bed and are lulled by trains passing in the night. Bob Jacobs' favorite spot is a balcony room on the second floor at the end of the hall; "It's a good train watching room," he said. About forty trains pass through Belton Station each day.

The beauty of the chalet, lodge, and cottages is in their simplicity. The key for Cas and Andy's restoration was to stay true to the buildings' spirit and integrity. Any additions made to accommodate modern plumbing, heating, or safety needs are so expertly crafted that they seem a part of the historic texture.

While the restoration was daunting, local support was not. As Cas Still recalled, "The community cheered us on. That was one of the things that kept us going."

Facing page: Belton's dormitory was restored into the main lodge and its lobby's simple charm was recaptured, top left. Guestrooms were reconfigured for the addition of private baths, but the original sinks remain in each room, top right. Each of the three-bedroom Lewis and Clark cottages features a sitting room with a fireplace, bottom. Nearly forty trains pass by Belton daily, and perfect vantage points from which to watch them are a rocker on the lodge balcony, right, or a cottage's front porch, below.

An historic red "Jammer" and Lake McDonald Lodge are both reminders of Glacier's past, above. The lodge was designed by Spokane architect, Kirtland Cutter, facing page.

LAKE McDONALD LODGE

OPENED 1914

Before Glacier was a national park in 1910, Louis Hill had been taken with Lake McDonald. The Great Northern Railway's station site at Belton was selected for easy access to Glacier's largest lake, and Hill had constructed a road from the station and Belton Chalet to the lake. But it would be John Lewis, a Montana businessman and fur trader from nearby Columbia Falls, who would construct the jewel on the shoreline.

In the 1890s, homesteaders settled on the shores of Lake McDonald, where they trapped game and considered other means of survival. In 1895, George Snyder built the Snyder Hotel on the present site of Lake McDonald Lodge. In 1904, John Lewis gained control of the Snyder Hotel and the 285 acres surrounding it. He envisioned more than his small fishing and tourist camp, a few homesteader cabins and the simple hotel on the pristine site. With Glacier designated a national park, he saw a niche for his own upgraded operation.

Lewis admired the alpine chalet design of Louis Hill's Belton Chalet and the grand Glacier Park Hotel, and if he couldn't fund something as large, at least he would equal its style. Lewis commissioned Kirtland Cutter of Spokane, Washington, to design his lodge.

Lake McDonald was a world away from the city environment where formal architecture thrived in the early 1900s. "The mountains, forests, and deserts of the West had been seen as an obstacle to America's progress, and people were only beginning to venture into them for pleasure," explained Henry Matthews, an architectural historian and Cutter's biographer. "American architecture, with its classical forms and aloofness from the land, had tended to symbolize the triumph of civilization over the wilderness. The idea of rustic architecture that would merge with mountainous landscape was entirely new."

In the late nineteenth century a few eastern tycoons built rustic summer "camps" tucked into the Adirondacks in upstate New York, but for most architects of the time, embracing Mother Nature was hardly natural.

To historian Matthews, those first Adirondack "camps" celebrating rusticity were "whimsical settings in which the very rich could play at being backwoodsmen, while

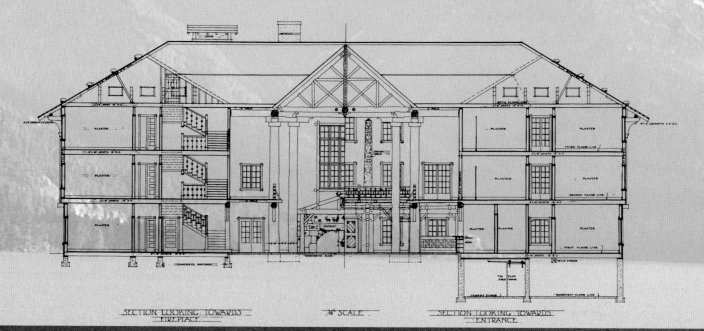

SECTION LOOKING TOWARDS FIREPLACE   ¼ SCALE   SECTION LOOKING TOWARDS ENTRANCE

A SWISS CHALET AND MONTANA HUNTING LODGE

GLACIER NATIONAL PARK, MONTANA

enjoying every possible luxury. And they were private places the public didn't see. Lodges in national parks could bring the enjoyment of rustic architecture to a much broader public."

Kirtland Cutter was comfortable with society's upper crust. Trained in New York and Europe as an artist, not a draftsman, he moved to Spokane at the urging of his uncle. The charming and gifted artist soon found his way into architecture, where he established a reputation for creating mansions for the Spokane elite. What set Cutter apart from the crowd was his interest in merging local building materials with his plans. His early work reflected the expanded English cottage style, and the era's Arts and Crafts movement.

Cutter's first significant experiment with rustic building and Swiss chalet motifs was not a private residence, but the very public Idaho Building he designed with his partner John Poetz for the 1893 World's Columbian Exposition in Chicago.

Boats such as the Cassie D, *above, brought guests to the Snyder Hotel. John Lewis acquired the site and built the exquisite Lake McDonald Lodge, top. Inside, the Swiss chalet transformed into a hunting lodge, facing page.*

"Cutter intended to evoke the pioneer spirit in the Idaho Building," observed Henry Matthews. "It was somewhat in the form of a Swiss chalet, but, built of immense tree trunks on a base of rough basalt, it evoked the grandeur of the forest. Some of the interior spaces were intended to replicate trappers' and miners' cabins. The Idaho Building captured the public imagination."

It also captured the imaginations of wealthy clients. Mrs. Lucy Carnegie commissioned Cutter to design an Adirondack camp in 1903. That was followed by a rustic summer retreat on Hayden Lake in Idaho. Both buildings followed the Swiss theme while embracing their wilderness surroundings.

But it would be in "America's Alps," as Louis Hill called the Rocky Mountains of Glacier, where Cutter would create the perfect alpine chalet while lassoing Montana rusticity.

Cutter had done preliminary drawings for Belton Chalet for Hill, and would do the same thing for Many Glacier Hotel, then watch the commissions go to railway architects. At Lake McDonald for Lewis, he would have the opportunity to finish what he began. Kirtland Cutter embarked on the uniquely American idea of a rustic yet elegant lodge in a national park.

Access to the hotel was part of its charm. Tourists arrived by train, then took a bumpy coach ride to the lake where they boarded steamboats for a cruise to docks in front of the hotel.

Today, guests can still take a cruise from the lodge aboard the *DeSmet,* a historic boat that originally brought visitors to the lodge. It was on the very route that materials to build the lodge were transported. With no road or rail access, building supplies were brought to the site by boat until the lake froze in the winter. Then supplies were skidded across the ice.

Concrete and foundation work were completed before the winter of 1913. The sixty-five-room hotel opened in June 1914 at a cost of $48,000. John Lewis named it the Lewis Glacier Hotel.

The main portion of the three-and-one-half-story structure is finished in a combination of white stucco and wood clapboarding painted the same brown as the Great Northern's hotels. Multiple balconies and jigsawn decorative bands of wood separate and define the floors. The same jigsawn detail frames windows and doors. Log columns support the first balcony, which has log railings and balustrades. On the lake side of the building, the bark remains on the post-and-beam balcony support. The gabled roof was originally topped, again in the traditional Swiss manner, with logs and stones. Deep eaves are supported by squared timbers with profiled ends.

"On the exterior, Cutter seemed unable to shake off the Swiss Chalet influence," observed Henry Matthews. "But, inside, the lobby is a totally original and awe inspiring space."

The center of that space is a three-story open great hall, perfectly square, with four corner columns each made from three large Western-cedar logs, which support the log floor structure of the balconies. Bark remains on the columns and much of the other log work, bringing the space to life. Anyone who comes to Lake McDonald Lodge is taken with the details that include two stairways with burled wood newel posts and jigsawn balustrades.

Within the forest interior, Cutter incorporated both Indian and pioneer spirits. Concrete floors are scored to look like flagstone, with incised

phrases in Blackfeet, Chippewa, and Cree ("welcome," "new life to those who drink here," "looking toward the mountain," and "big feast"). Balconies that bank the open lobby on three sides feature bark-covered cedar log

The open stairway off the lobby features burled newel posts and sapling balustrades.

railings and balustrades. Cutter, who was not fond of the skylights at Glacier Park Lodge, let the sun shine in through a two-story paned window above the fireplace. The huge hearth is framed by Indian designs scored and painted around the opening. Montana artist Charles Russell, a friend of Lewis and his wife, was a frequent visitor to the lodge. Speculation is that Russell inspired the fireplace designs.

Lewis was an avid traveler, collector, and hunter; elk, antelope, moose, goat, eagle, and mountain sheep trophies hung on the columns and walls, and animal skins and Navajo rugs were draped from the balconies. Frank Stick, John Fery, and H. Bartlett oil paintings, and Fred Kiser photographs, filled the walls. Artists, tourists, and trappers swapped stories in the lobby.

Guestrooms were off both sides of the lobby and on the upper floors. A separate wing to the lobby's south housed the dining room and kitchen, offering everything tourists required: a place to eat and sleep, and a perfect hunting lodge "salon" in which to socialize.

"Lake McDonald Lodge is such a unique blend of rustic, Swiss, [and] Indian motifs and an element of Japanese tea house. It had all of these themes that blended together, that they felt comfortable with," marveled National Park Service historical architect Paul Newman.

While arriving at the remote lodge by boat was charming, Lewis understood the changing times, and lobbied for a road. The Great Northern was building roads in East Glacier, but politics bogged down west-side road development. In 1919, Lewis built three and a half miles of road on the eastern side of Lake McDonald with his own funds. Lewis's initial $3,200 investment provided an important link of what would become the $3 million Going-to-the-Sun Highway (now Road), which was officially opened in July 1933.

In 1920, road work continued under park jurisdiction, and by the late summer of 1921, rough road access was completed to Lewis Glacier Hotel, and guests began arriving through the "back door." A balcony was added and the back was spruced up as the new entrance. Now, with guests entering from both sides of the building, the original design began to lose its integrity.

Lewis and representatives of the Great Northern (GN) had an ongoing rivalry, and by 1929 pressure was on John Lewis and his wife to sell their hotel. The GN's Glacier Park Hotel Company was interested in buying out Lewis, who was becoming increasingly difficult to deal with as they organized their trail and chalet trips. Negotiations "looked like a riot" wrote railway representative James Maher when he offered Lewis $250,000 for the hotel and land.

On January 13, 1930, Ralph Budd of GN's Glacier Park Hotel Company wrote NPS Director Horace Albright concerning the sale: "He [Lewis] is a queer kind of man, and one of the best things to convince him will be for him to get an official notice some way that the road is not going to be finished under the present conditions. He is one of the hardest men in the world to deal with, and it is going to be difficult to get this across, but I think we can get him this year. We are going to re-open the Belton Chalets, and by some means convince him that he is foolish to continue to run the hotel."

Lewis sold the hotel to the National Park Service in 1930 in a complicated financial deal that included the Great Northern Railway. Glacier Park Hotel Company became the concessionaire and, anxious to eliminate all reminders of Lewis, they changed the name to Lake McDonald Hotel (later Lake McDonald Lodge).

The lodge was restored as part of a $1.2 million project that included bringing back the dining room's original charm.

Over the years, a flood, reconfiguration, and remodeling bore down on the structure and eroded its character. As times changed, a gift shop, offices, suitcase storage, and a registration desk encroached on the impressive lobby. Sitting in the midst of the once idyllic lobby was no longer a pleasant experience.

"One of the obscene things done," as architect Newman saw it, "was to enlarge the gift shop so they changed the access from the lobby down a corridor through the dining room. It had been quite dramatic, but when they enlarged the gift shop they lost that original axis—lost that whole feeling of procession into one of the most wonderful dining rooms."

Outside, dirty laundry was tossed or hung from the windows on the lodge's lake side. "Sheets and laundry would pile ten feet high every single day. That's an awful way to deal with the building and the landscape," continued Newman.

That changed in 1988-1989 when Lake McDonald Lodge underwent a $1.2 million rehabilitation.

The project goal was twofold: to restore the flavor, integrity, and details of the 1914 construction and bring back the ambiance lost over time, and to meet accessibility requirements.

Paul Newman became the project manager: "At that point, it looked more like a Denny's than a historic lodge."

The crew sunk the registration desk into the edge of the lobby in what used to be a guestroom, and moved other services that cluttered the space, thus restoring the original circulation pattern. Damaged cedar logs or bark were replaced and the infrastructure upgraded. Historical paint analyses revealed the original terra cotta paint and stencil pattern, which was restored. The fabulous fireplace and inglenook were cleaned and renovated. A remodeled gift shop, cocktail lounge, relocated restrooms, and accessible guestrooms were incorporated.

Unlike in other Glacier Park lodges, many original hunting trophies and pieces of furniture remained here. Some of the hickory chairs, notably those with thick log legs and arms, or cane seats, are historic. The lobby's large oak table with cedar-bark–covered base, and the huge slab table in the south corner are original, as are the upright piano and scalloped-back chairs. Reproductions, including many hickory pieces from the Old Hickory Furniture Company, of Indiana, were ordered, and lobby rugs were designed and woven to match the colors and patterns of original Gustav Stickley area rugs. A group of Roycroft crafters produced three couches to look like the originals.

The distinctive shades hanging in the lobby and dining room were originally painted by the Blood Indians and hung in the Prince of Wales Hotel in Waterton Lakes National Park, Canada. In the 1960s, they were moved to Lake McDonald, and in 1982, Montana artist Kay Storms was commissioned to reproduce the deteriorating shades using the original framework.

Besides bringing back the rustic feel of the décor and much of the integrity of Cutter's design, the renovation uncovered some of the lodge's history.

The dining room—nearly wiped out in a 1964 flood that tore through Snyder Creek—was one such story. Architectural drawings for the dining wing were never found, only Cutter's connection plans to the room. According to Paul Newman, the dining room was constructed from an assemblage of on-site buildings. A larger log building is the center of the structure, with two log cabins hooked together to create additional dining space and the kitchen wing. Renovation work revealed a foundation that was not the same quality as the rest of the building. However the room was assembled, when complete the original dining room created a strong axis terminating at the fireplace.

Now guests are drawn into the dining room as they enter an intimate upper level dining space, then follow steps into the main room. The fireplace, focal point at the far end of the room, was rebuilt from local river stone. The walls, replaced after the flood with studs and plywood, were restored with squared cedar logs, each one individually hand-worked to replicate the originals. Hardwood floors complement the wood furniture (about sixty percent of which is original). At night, the room glows from the light of hand-painted shades and Arts and Crafts period sconces.

The roadside entrance was made more inviting by eliminating the dirt berm, gently terracing the grade and taking out the steep stairs. Cracked stucco on crumbling brick and rotted wood was replaced. One of the finishing touches was to restore a lodge icon. Lewis had acquired a totem pole on his travels to southeastern Alaska, and while the pole was long gone, photographs of it were analyzed and a replica commissioned from an Alaskan carver.

On the lake side of the lodge, in addition to the original porch lined with hickory rockers, new terraces and seating areas, and walkways to the boat docks, now unify lake and lodge. Native stone was used for the walls, and the same technique of scored concrete used in the lobby was repeated outdoors. The grounds are landscaped with native plants; annuals fill the baskets and planters as they did in 1914.

Renovation began on October 14, 1988, but it was not to be an easy project. Weather was typical—snow depths of two feet and temperatures from ninety degrees to minus thirty degrees. It wasn't the Arctic wind or snow that stopped construction, but the American bald eagle. Prior to construction work, National Park Service naturalists had advised the crew that construction could not disturb migratory or nesting eagles. Hence, the contract called for fifty-four days in which construction would cease, and fifty-six were specified for only night work. From November 20 to December 31, 1988, no work of any type was allowed at the site, and from March 18 through April 23, 1989, only night work was allowed. The lodge opened for operation that season, and detail work was completed over the summer.

In 1987 the lodge was designated a National Historic Landmark. It remains under the ownership of the U.S. government and jurisdiction of the National Park Service, and is operated by a private concessionaire.

Besides the lodge, the Lake McDonald Historic District includes a cluster of cabins built between 1907 and 1908. These have been updated over time and are rented to guests. The entire complex has a camp village atmosphere with dorms, first-aid station, general store, and an auditorium/chapel. A family-style restaurant, built during the NPS Mission 66 phase, is functional but out of character with the area and is an example of what might have happened to the architecture of the district if expansion plans had been completed at that time.

One need look no farther than the small rise where Lake McDonald Lodge stands for rustic alpine architectural inspiration. "It surpasses the other lodges at Glacier," explained Paul Newman. "Lake McDonald Lodge may not be as grand as the other Glacier Park hotels, but the detail is spectacular."

An Alaskan totem pole based on the original stands at the road-side entry of the lodge, right. The chalet design with wide eaves supported by corbeled log brackets, crisp white jigsawn trim, and balconies with log railings, stands in contrast to one of the original log cabins, below.

Granite Park Chalet, a small stone token of the past, is silhouetted against the Livingston Range, above. Photos like the one taken at Sperry in 1939, facing page, publicized the backcountry chalet experience.

SPERRY & GRANITE PARK CHALETS

1913 & 1915

Swiss-style chalets and teepee camps all linked by bridle and hiking trails once dotted the far reaches of Glacier National Park. Louis Hill, president of the Great Northern Railway, challenged tourists who had previously traveled to Europe to "See America First." To entice them to the wilds of Montana he recreated the European model with a network of luxury hotels and backcountry retreats. At the end of a day of hiking or riding, tourists found the comfort of charming shelter and a warm meal in breathtaking settings.

The chalets may have looked Swiss, but the wranglers who led horse-packing parties over the Rockies to them were not. This was indeed the America West.

Most of the original nine chalets built by the Great Northern, beginning in 1911 with the construction of Two Medicine Chalet complex, are gone. The Great Northern's holdings closed down during World War II, and the majority of the chalets never reopened. Instead, in 1949 most of the chalets were razed; some buildings burned and one was leveled by an avalanche. Sperry and Granite Park chalets, constructed of stone and timber, fared better than most and continued to operate. But in 1992, Sperry and Granite Park chalets were closed because of safety and environmental concerns. The park service asked for public comment on their fate. They got it from both sides. Eventually, it was decided that Sperry and Granite Park chalets would not follow the fate of Cutbank, St. Mary or Going-to-the-Sun chalets.

In 1995, then Superintendent David Mihalic announced that Granite Park would be restored and reopened as a self-service alpine shelter overseen by the NPS, and Sperry would follow as a full-service chalet. In a partnership between the public and the private sector, money was raised for the restoration. The summer of 1996 was when the first visitors returned to Granite Park, and in 1999 the restored Sperry Chalet housed guests and served meals in the Great Northern tradition. The past was alive again.

Hiking trails lead to both chalets, and at Sperry guests can ride in on horseback as in the days when Glacier was called a "horse packer's

park." Riders swing into their saddles at Mule Shoe Outfitters at Lake McDonald. Wranglers check them out for the six-and-a-half-mile ride. "We'll climb thirty-seven hundred feet at six percent grade," explained Bruce Jacobs, who has been "cowboying" for fifty years. "I've literally been on horseback all my life from the time I was six weeks when my parents would tie a sweater around me and put me on their backs and away we'd go."

Jacobs has been packing in supplies and leading guests to Sperry Chalet each season. "The experience is something you'll never get anywhere in the world. It's gorgeous and spectacular. We take you from our corrals surrounded by cedar forest, through trees about a hundred-fifty feet high, then above timberline and you cross a river—twice," he said of the three-and-a-half-hour trip. "The chalet sits right on the edge of a cliff. One of the most prettiest places you'll see."

"A jewel," stated Laura Jo Measure about Sperry Chalet, where she hiked for forty consecutive years. "Lovely. Not as you would suppose most jewels would be, but a jewel to me," said the ninety-one-year-old Montana native who began a writing career when she was seventy-five.

To people like Measure the pleasure of a Sperry experience is threefold: the buildings that remain much as they were when "Mr. Hill and his Italian stoneworkers built them," the challenge of hiking there, and the setting perched on the edge of a glacier-caved cirque. As Jo Measure explained it: "They are beautiful buildings, and the way they're situated with the mountains it enhances the beauty. But you have to test your

Hiking or packing into Sperry is part of its lasting appeal, left, where little seems to have changed—including the Great Northern Railway (GNRy) letters in the gable—since this 1930s photo, below.

strength against the mountain to really appreciate it. I love those trails. If heaven is anything like that, I won't miss Earth."

The chalet is really two lovely stone structures. A two-story dormitory now sleeps forty-two guests in private rooms, and guests take meals at a separate kitchen/dining chalet. It was probably the expert work of Italian stone masons that gave the buildings foundations enabling them to survive decades of Montana winters. Not only is the stone work of high quality, but the rugged randomness of the design also gives it perfect context in the sub-alpine setting. The shingle roof, dormers with small wood balconies off the second floor, and arched lintels over

windows and doors all come together in creating the perfect backcountry retreat. The dormitory designed by Samuel L. Bartlett (Glacier Park Lodge) in 1913 and the Dining Hall designed by Thomas McMahon (Many Glacier Hotel and Prince of Wales Hotel) in 1915 both feature high-mountain alpine architecture.

Initial cost estimates for the Sperry buildings were $11,400, but when completed, the complex cost the Great Northern close to $30,000. With its spectacular setting overlooking Lake McDonald Valley and the Whitefish Range, Sperry was an immediate success. The chalet was named after Dr. Lyman B. Sperry, who had been asked by Great Northern agents to observe possible scenic attractions beginning in 1894.

Restored but not modernized, it has no electricity, plumbing, or heat; heavy wool blankets cut the night chill, and battery- or propane-operated lamps offer their humble glow. A bowl and pitcher is in each room, and a state-of-the-art "comfort station" is nearby. Meals are prepared on propane stoves and served family style for breakfast and dinner. A la carte or trail lunches are offered, and day hikers stop by for refreshment.

The chalet camps began with dining and recreation chalets surrounded by floored tents later replaced with either cabins or dorms. Both Granite Park and Sperry offered dormitory sleeping. The high elevation and lack of water were two initial objections to the Granite Park site, but permission for the ten-acre site was granted in 1912. The smaller dormitory was designed by Thomas McMahon and built in 1913; the larger two-story chalet was constructed in 1914 as designed by Samuel L. Bartlett.

The Glacier Park Company, a subsidiary to the Great Northern Railway, recorded building progress at its hotels and chalets, listing names

of influential guests in their monthly bulletins.

The bulletins also documented the construction progress. While most the chalet camps were closing up for the season, at Granite Park construction continued but it was slow going. On September 12, 1914, manager J.A. Shoemaker reported that four feet of snow was up the one-story walls, and that the crew was out shoveling snow from the trail for two days and working at the stone quarry when possible. "Rain and snow every day past week. Only three pack trains up," he wrote in the terse report.

Granite Park Chalet opened in 1915 on the edge of a sub-alpine meadow with views of Lake McDonald Valley, the Livingston Range with a prominent view of Heavens Peak, and the southwest portion of the park. Stone walls, wood shingles on the exterior, and flagstone floors and vertical log partitions and log framing, created simple but charming shelter. The dormitory is built of the same rubble stone with a shingle roof, with slightly arched lintels in keeping with the larger chalet and the more elegant hotels of the Great Northern development.

Today, Granite Park serves as a hiker's stopover, with room and beds provided. Guests pack in their own food, sleeping bags, and water filters. An optional linen/bedding and packaged meal service is available.

Both backcountry chalets, now National Historic Landmarks, offer a unique opportunity to experience the park. The chalets and trails were how Louis Hill wanted the park to be seen, how he meant it to be seen.

"We're connected to the world whether we want to be or not," said Laura Jo Measure as she recalled her hikes to Sperry and Granite Park. That connection lives at the surviving backcountry chalets of Glacier National Park.

The backcountry chalets were popular with "dudes," and during the Twenties and Thirties log additions housed guests at Granite Park Chalet, above. While the additions have been removed, much remains the same, including packing in supplies for this high country retreat, right.

The best way to see Many Glacier Hotel is from Swiftcurrent Lake, above. Kirtland Cutter's preliminary drawings, facing page, were not the final word on the hotel's design.

MANY GLACIER HOTEL

OPENED 1915

It is called "Many" by the legions of people who love it.

The third hotel constructed by Louis Hill and the Great Northern Railway in Glacier National Park, its massive hulk is softened by scallops, cupolas, balconies, and dormers.

Louis Hill picked the site for the hotel in 1909 in a pocket of glacial carving and erosion along the shore of Swiftcurrent Lake. It is a place where one is seemingly locked in by the geography. Out "there" in the wilds were the bear, deer, beavers, and fowl. Inside, the animals were stuffed, and the beauty man-made. While larger than its counterpart in East Glacier, Many Glacier Hotel, built like a series of chalets, is set in the midst of such natural grandeur that it seems slightly less daunting.

The best way to understand the relationship of Many Glacier Hotel to Glacier Park is by boat. *Chief Two Guns,* a wooden craft built in 1961, leaves the dock in front of the hotel and chugs across Swiftcurrent Lake on its early morning excursion. There one is caught between two worlds, to the east the Swiss-inspired building and to the west the mountains that can only humble it.

Art Burch, Jr., is from the third generation of the family that established Glacier Park Boat Company. Dew still clings to the dock as passengers gingerly step aboard for the first cruise of the day. Art welcomes guests with the same

Montana hospitality his grandfather used in 1938, when he bought the operation. Art introduces himself and, as the boat pulls onto the lake, Many Glacier Hotel comes into focus.

"The Many Glacier, with two hundred and twelve rooms, is largest of the hotels built by Louis Hill and the Great Northern Railway," explains Art Burch over the drone of the engine. "Louis Hill wanted to increase the number of visitors to the park, and he embarked on an ambitious project that included hotels, chalets and roads."

As the story unfolds, "Many" settles into the landscape. "The Many Glacier is the most remote hotel, and construction began in September 1914. A crew of two hundred men was brought up here; experienced carpenters, they worked throughout the winter months and had the hotel ready to open July 4, 1915."

Hill provided some of the crew for that long winter construction and Evensta & Company of

Minneapolis was selected as the contractor. Thomas McMahon drew on his earlier experience of designing Glacier Park Lodge with Samuel L. Barlett, and the work of Kirtland Cutter, to design a four-and-one-half story hotel in three separate structures.

Hill and Ralph Budd, acting president of the Great Northern while Hill devoted his time to the Glacier projects, both courted Spokane architect Kirtland Cutter to provide plans for the site. John Lewis had hired Cutter to design the exquisite Lake McDonald Lodge (then called Lewis Glacier Hotel) that opened in June 1914. Hill, Cutter, and Thomas McMahon visited the park in the spring of 1914, and both architects proceeded with preliminary plans. Cutter submitted at least two sets of pencil-sketch plans and blueprints. But Hill wasn't satisfied, and by July, noted in correspondence, "We have not the plans perfected yet and will not do anything on this building this year." By early fall, Hill decided to use McMahon as the architect. A disappointed Cutter billed the Great Northern Railway $1,000 "for services rendered." Hill reluctantly paid, and McMahon proceeded.

The Swiss chalet architecture combined with timbers and native rock—a hallmark of Cutter's Lake McDonald Lodge, the Idaho Building for which he won a gold medal at the 1893 World's Columbian Exposition in Chicago, and his own home in Spokane—is prevalent at Many

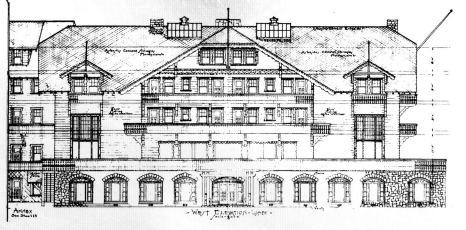

FRAGILE REMINDER OF THE PAST
GLACIER NATIONAL PARK, MONTANA

With the completion of an eighty-six-room annex in 1917, the hotel cost $500,000 to construct in this remote location, right. Glacier was always known as a "packer's" park, and horses lined up at the hitching posts in 1931, above. Today, visitors often arrive in vans with bicycle tour groups ready to ride through the park, facing page.

Glacier. Cutter's Many Glacier elevation drawing from the lakeside shows the lobby turned to face the lake, first-floor stonework with arched windows, tiered balconies, and a gabled roof topped with a cupola. With the exception of the cupola, McMahon incorporated these designs in his plans. Eventually two cupolas were built atop two later additions: the breezeway and porte-cochere.

Even with its Swiss chalet architecture, Many Glacier Hotel is built primarily of native material. While the great hall is basically the same as that of Glacier Park Lodge, Many Glacier's hall is half the size. Once again, the massive single support timbers were brought from the Pacific Northwest by the Great Northern to East Glacier Station, then hauled by horse to the building site. Other timber was harvested from the Grinnell Lake area, then carried by floats across Lake Josephine and Swiftcurrent Lake. A sawmill was set up for the project on site, where Hill also built a planing mill and kiln. (A decade later, Stephen Mather, director of the National Park Service, would have the mill dynamited in a show of pique and power after Hill refused to follow his orders to demolish it.)

While Hill waited for timber permits, excavation, and stone and preparatory work were taking place at the site; there was hardly a lull in development. By the time construction began, eight of the nine chalets in his grand plan had been completed.

The hotel was the main structure in a group of buildings proposed for the site. By December, framing was up for the dormitory, and stone foundation for the main hotel had been laid. Stone for that foundation, and the waterfront terrace with its segmental arched windows and doors, was quarried from the area. McMahon was pleased. "The stone in this foundation comes practically square...it was laid as it came from the mountain," he relayed to Hill in December 1914. Buried deep in the Montana winter, by January Great Northern bridge builders had put the forty-foot timbers in place for the lobby, and the dormitory wing, bridge, and dining room were under construction.

"They were under extreme conditions," explained National Park Service (NPS) architect Gayle Burgess, who has been involved with the planning and design for the hotel's rehabilitation that began in the fall of 2001. "As project supervisor who has spent a great deal of time on construction sites, I cannot help but think about what they had to deal with during construction—the remoteness of location, the severe weather conditions." And Burgess pointed out that construction typical of that period was not intended to last over twenty-five years, and workers may have been rushed so they could get out of the weather: "It's understandable that some construction details are coming back to haunt 'Many'." Still, her admiration is not dampened. "I applaud their efforts. Without their persistence, 'Many' would not be here today. They're my heroes."

One of the multitude of challenges faced by the crew due to its remote location was transporting timbers from Glacier Park Station to the site over fifty miles away. Logs are without bark, and whether the timbers were peeled because the bark was damaged during the trip to the site, or logged too late in the season, is unknown. So, instead of the rustic log balustrades and railings of Glacier Park Lodge, hand-carved balustrades bring the chalet look of the Many Glacier exterior inside. Three balconies line two sides of the lobby with guestrooms off them; the third floor (crow's nest) is used as employee housing. A stairway is at each end of the lobby. Board and batten wainscoting with

white fiberboard above add to the Swiss theme.

When Many Glacier opened it had the feeling of a hybrid hunting lodge. The heavy Swiss motif—down to the red and white Greek crosses on guestroom doors—or the Japanese lanterns hanging from the wooden rafters and umbrellas secured in logs on the orange floor of the great hall, didn't overshadow the Western theme. Buffalo skulls, some made of plaster of Paris, and over a dozen silvertip (grizzly) bear skins hung from the balconies. A moose head above the gift shop is all that remains of the lobby's original hunting trophies. (The ram in the lobby

was the victim of a fall through the skylight one winter.) A 180-foot mural, painted in panels by Blackfeet artists, covered an entire wall. Totem poles (seven were ordered from the Pacific Northwest) dotted the lobby.

Hill chose a variety of seemingly "disposable" furniture to fill the lobby: dozens of Japanese wicker, Windsor, and canvas-folding chairs cluttered the room. As spring of 1915 approached, Hill was busy ordering everything from checker and chess sets to bundles of bamboo fishing poles for decorating the Grill Room.

In 1940, the great hall still featured the spiral stairway and rock fountain, left. The dining room originally had an open ceiling festooned with lanterns and parasols, below.

A miniature mountain was created at the south end of the great hall. The spiral stairway that led down to the Bamboo Room wound around a fountain built from native rock and decorated with ferns. Colored lights shone on the fountain and trout swam in the pond at its base. Music from dance bands downstairs rose into the lobby, one of the reasons given for the fountain's removal in 1957. More likely, this was to expand the gift shop twenty feet into the lobby, with a stuffed ram sitting atop its front wall. A firepit still stands at the lobby's north end, its huge copper hood suspended over the native stone base where a fire burns each day and night. A rustic stone fireplace is near the entrance, along with over a dozen others in the hotel, all nonfunctioning today.

The dining room at Many Glacier is not off the great hall as is the usual lodge floor plan. Instead, diners meander down a corridor of guestrooms, through a breezeway (now the Interlaken Lounge) to the Ptarmigan Dining Room. Anchored by a huge stone fireplace, the room is blessed with floor-to-ceiling windows along the west wall and on each side of the fireplace. Original John Fery paintings commissioned by Hill hang at the dining room entrance.

As with Glacier Park Lodge, the new hotel did not meet the need for rooms. An eighty-room annex was completed in 1917, and as construction prices climbed, Hill demanded an accounting report that compared the recently completed Paradise Inn at Mount Rainier, Washington (Hill thought it had been built for $40,000) to Many Glacier Hotel. "They seem to have some economical way of doing this work," Hill noted in an October 16 memo to Ralph Budd. McMahon complied and provided a comparative study. It was obvious the Great Northern was building a much larger, far more luxurious and sophisticated structure, and one

While the stairway and fountain were removed, the "campfire" fireplace still warms the towering space of the great hall, left. A false ceiling was put in the dining room where guests enjoy spectacular views, above.

much farther from any metropolitan area than the Paradise Inn. When completed, Many Glacier Hotel featured steam heat, electric lights, hot and cold water, and an indoor plunge pool—at a total cost of $500,000.

The exterior is "national park brown" with yellow jigsawn trim and white window frames. The roofline is a variety of gables, many finished with clipped-gable ends. Long dormers and hip roofs are finished with wood shingles.

Like that of any historic building, "Many's" story is not without high drama. On August 31, 1936, one of Montana's forest fires suddenly broke through fire lines and raced toward the Swiftcurrent Valley and Many Glacier Hotel. Guests were evacuated by bus. The fire engulfed four chalets as it moved toward Swiftcurrent Lake. Burning forest debris flew across the lake and hit the hotel, but the main blaze blew around it. Staff fought the flames and saved the structure, then in jubilation of their feat, wired the Great Northern headquarters: "WE HAVE SAVED THE HOTEL!" By then the hotels were losing propositions for the railway; the terse telegram reply read: "WHY?"

In the 1950s, the Great Northern spent $1.5 million sprucing up their hotel holdings to sell them. Many Glacier was the main target for "renovation." Linoleum tile covered the original hardwood (now carpeted) floors, the spiral stairway was removed, several guestrooms were eliminated next to the breezeway, and the Swiss Lounge was constructed. Much of the work detracted from the historic integrity of the building, but the Swiss Lounge reflects the same detail the railroad was known for. Outside the lounge are two Charles de Feo oil paintings.

In 1960, the hotels were acquired by Glacier Park, Inc., whose president Don Hummel ran them for twenty years, selling the operation to Greyhound Corporation (now Viad Corp) in 1981. But not before a group of former employees formed Glacier Park Foundation and attempted to purchase the hotel.

"Glacier Park Foundation is a kitchen table organization—entirely volunteer," said John Hagen, a Minneapolis attorney and foundation president. "Employees formed a nonprofit with the hope to go into partnership with private investors. Our concept would have paid off the private investors over time and run the conces-

sion on a nonprofit basis." Unable to put together a sufficiently capitalized bid, they saw their offer rejected, but the organization remains as a citizen group devoted to public interest in Glacier Park and the visitor services.

So much that makes "Many" special is the personal attachment of those who have stayed or worked there. Tessie Bundick first came to "Many" as a college student from Texas in 1972. "Every morning you woke up to this extraordinary beautiful panorama from that hotel. And it was yours—all yours. It had the romance of the West, the romance of the railroad days, the romance of the theatre. Tons of young interesting people who were excited to be alive worked there. There was no TV, no newspapers. We were out of touch with the real world. We were in an enchanted place. And we knew it."

From 1961 through 1983, "Many" was the venue for Broadway musicals, nightly hootenannies, serenades, concerts, or dances to the music of a combo band. All were performed by music, drama, and theater majors from around the country, who also worked as maids, waiters and bellboys. The cavalcade of entertainment was the inspiration of Ian Tippet, a tall, elegant Englishman who, as the concessionaire's director of human resources, set out to make guests' "Many" experience one they would fondly remember. While the hotel was charming, it had physical problems including banging steam pipes from the erratic heating system, thin guestroom walls, and only half its rooms offering much-sought lake views. The answer came in the entertainment. "Guests forgot about the pipes or if their room was too hot. Instead, they were enraptured by the spirit of the whole thing," recalled Mr. Tippet.

Designated a National Historic Landmark in 1987, today the Many Glacier Hotel complex

belongs to the National Park Service, and a private concessionaire has a compensable interest in the facilities, owns its furnishings, and manages the hotel. Hundreds of thousands of dollars have been spent over the years on maintenance and upkeep (including solving the heating and pipe problems), but millions are needed to restore it.

In 1996, Many Glacier, along with other Glacier Park buildings, was included in the National Trust for Historic Preservation's list of "America's 11 Most Endangered Historic Places." At that time, an estimate for its basic rehabilitation was $30 million.

In 2001, after decades of neglect, steps were taken to stabilize and restore Many Glacier Hotel by addressing its foundation. Straightening a basement hallway (for years called "stagger alley") was part of the project.

"I don't know how I can describe it," Gayle Burgess explained of the years of neglect. "It's been the orphan child. Part of that is it's just a huge building. A series of Band-Aids can't fix it. Our goal is to raise it back to glory again."

Park superintendent Suzanne Lewis emphasized, "It's not about making it pretty, it's not about making it perfect. To me it's about insuring that it's absolutely there for every generation to come."

Eight decades after Many Glacier Hotel was built, Hill's genius in bringing together the wilds of Glacier National Park and their visitors remains.

"We're here to try to connect people," explained Superintendent Lewis, "and the lodges go a long way to providing that connection. Whether your interest is natural history or scenery or whatever in the park, these hotels are our connection to our past and our connection to the future. This is so vital, so deep-rooted, we don't want to lose them."

Canoes stand ready for tourists to glide across Swiftcurrent Lake, top left, where Mount Wilbur, left, is juxtaposed with the hotel's annex. The cupola-topped breezeway links the main hotel and annex, top right.

The Prince of Wales Hotel was the Great Northern Railway's final hotel as part of its Glacier development, above. Thomas McMahon designed the hotel with a Canadian rather than U.S. western sensibility, facing page.

PRINCE OF WALES HOTEL

OPENED 1927

Louis Hill picked the windswept knoll above Upper Waterton Lake in 1913 for the final link in the Great Northern Railway's chain of resorts. The site became the pedestal for the whimsical chateau.

The idea for his hotel that would link Glacier National Park in Montana with Waterton Lakes in Alberta, Canada, had languished for a decade. During that time, World War I broke out; Canada, and then the United States, joined the war effort. In 1919, the Canadian government debated a proposal to dam the narrows between Upper and Middle Waterton Lakes. By 1921, the idea for a dam died, and Hill's hotel plans were reborn. But the focus and drive that was the hallmark of Glacier National Park development had faded in fifteen years. Hill's vision not only wavered, but also reached peaks and troughs as dramatic as the future hotel's surrounding landscape.

New government and park regulations and Hill's gnawing fear that visitors might never get to this little bit of wilderness were as real as the sometimes-inaccessible roads to Waterton. Hill secured a land lease from the Canadian government in February 1926, and established the Canadian Rockies Hotel Company, Limited. Plans were announced that same month that the Great Northern would build a 450-room hotel for $500,000.

Thomas McMahon was commissioned to draw plans, thinking this would be a replica of his design of Many Glacier Hotel. In May, Hill told McMahon to halt plans, and then withdrew funds until he felt assured that the roads would be completed to the hotel. Constructing Many Glacier Hotel far from the main rail line had been a challenge, and Waterton was even more remote. By the time Hill got the road issue "resolved," the architect was already a month behind schedule.

In July 1926, Douglas Oland and James Scott of Oland Scott Construction in Cardston, Alberta, were contracted to build the hotel.

Within days, they had a crew ready to work. Their deadline: July 1, 1927. As Oland prepared the site, McMahon rushed on with the plans. Oland and Scott were accomplished builders, but the Prince of Wales project would be the biggest and most complex structure of the company's history. Oland threw himself into the project, working sixteen hours a day. In his handwritten memoirs, Oland recounts his early problems with finding a reliable foreman, the lack of equipment, and the deterioration of the dirt roads. "Another drawback was the lack of good equipment, especially hoisting equipment [for] all the many timbers used, and there were a lot, [they] were hoisted by horse power. There was no good excavating equipment to get south of Calgary and the soil where I dug the basement was all large boulders in clay." The rocks weighed from 100 to 400 pounds each.

Building had started late in the season, and while the foundation work was well underway by August, exactly how the completed hotel would look was undecided. Hill called in Toltz King and Day of St. Paul as consulting architects. As Hill and Max Toltz came up with more elaborate plans, Great Northern executives in St. Paul, Minnesota, were thinking smaller. The proposed 450-room hotel had already been downsized to 300 rooms, and now that was shrunk to sixty-five rooms. At the site,

PERCHED ON A PEDESTAL
WATERTON LAKES NATIONAL PARK, ALBERTA, CANADA

September rain had made the roads impassable by truck, and Oland was hauling freight by horse and wagon. Soon snow was falling. Framing began and the hotel took shape through October, but by the end of the month, Oland had laid off half his building crew. The railway's field accountant, George Anderegg, continued filing weekly reports. Timber, lumber, cement, shingles, brick, and loads of other supplies were at the site. The plans were not.

Hill was touring France and Switzerland, and when he saw something he liked, his photographer would take the picture and send it back to McMahon, and the architect would again change the plans. McMahon's original concept of a four-story structure was revised to a seven-story, whimsical dollhouse. According to Oland's memoirs, "This meant that a lot of the structure as it now stands, had to be rebuilt four times, in early December I had walls and roof all framed, and this had to be torn down to the first floor." A fifth floor was added to the two wings, increasing guestrooms from sixty-five to ninety.

The hotel reinforced the Swiss chalet motif of the Great Northern's Glacier hotels, and at the same time attempted to defy nature by extending the knoll into an architectural landmark. Wind studies had been done on the site, but defiance of the one-hundred-mile-per-hour gusts was almost the hotel's downfall.

In December, building was going as planned and the hotel was taking shape, built in sections. The two wings were enclosed and covered with scaffolding. On December 10, a storm blew into Waterton. Workers battened down loose material—then the wind took over. According to Oland's memoirs, the resident engineer estimated readings of an average of eighty-four miles per hour with gusts of one hundred miles per hour. "I would not have been too greatly surprised if the whole building had blown down, as it was, it blew eight inches off plumb," wrote Oland. Timber from the site landed two miles away. Oland's crew winched the structure back within four inches of its original spot. "After that I put a lot of extra bracing in that was not called for in the plans," he wrote.

Snowstorms, a second major windstorm, and the deterioration of existing roads plagued the project. When trucks couldn't deliver supplies, sleighs did the job. When even sleighs or horses couldn't get through the usual route, Scott found another road.

Oland became more determined to complete the job as close to deadline as possible. Crews steadily increased, from sixty in mid-January to ninety by the end of February, and to 125 in April. When the Great Northern recommended postponing the opening until the 1928 season, it was Douglas Oland who objected. He wrote that if they would guarantee delivery of the material and quit changing the plans, he would "give them the hotel." By June 22, 225 men were on

The great hall's columns and beams are hand hewn rather than the logs used in Glacier, and Indian pictographs once decorated the walls, below. Décor may change, but not the view framed in the great hall windows, left. Today, the dining room looks very much like it did when the hotel opened in 1927, facing page.

site, and the hotel was ninety-one percent complete, according to Anderegg's weekly report. On July 25, 1927, fifteen days after Oland and Scott predicted, the Prince of Wales Hotel opened. The cost was $300,000.

What had developed on the hill overlooking Waterton Lakes was the largest wood structure in Alberta. As with the Glacier hotels, the great timbers were transported by rail from the Pacific Northwest to Glacier Park Station, then moved by truck, horse, or sleigh to the site.

The hotel's seven-story core features the great hall lobby flanked by two five-story wings and a single-story kitchen annex. Peaked dormers and tiers of bracketed balconies cascade down the upper levels of the steeply pitched, gabled roofs. A cupola and weathervane top the design. Unlike the other Great Northern lodges, the huge interior timbers are all peeled and hand-planed. Originally, the cedar roof was meant to weather. It was painted in the 1950s and replaced in 1994 with a dark green, fireproof composite tile roof. The contrasting exterior paint emphasizes the structural detail.

Eighteen-foot-high windows along the lake-view side of the great hall frame a scene that none of the artists Hill hired to promote the hotels could capture.

The great hall is far more refined than its Glacier counterparts. The architecture of the Canadian parks was rustic-Tudor, while to the south the rusticity reflected the "Wild West." The interior of Prince of Wales features the Tudor theme. The columns and trusses that fill the lobby are all hand-hewn, and the wood is fitted and pegged together. Iron butterfly hinges and plates reinforce the joists. A second-floor balcony fills two sides of the lobby with jigsawn balustrades. Each floor has a balustrade balcony or windows from the stairs that lead to the upper-floor attic rooms.

Louis Hill had a long-standing respect for the Blackfeet Indians around Glacier, and he asked the elders of the Blood Indian tribe to paint pictographs that filled the lobby. Hand-painted lanterns with the same Indian designs hung from the rafters.

The Prince of Wales Hotel's interior has been reinvented over time, mostly in the 1950s during the time the railway was renovating its hotels with hopes of selling. The Indian pictographs were removed and some of the lanterns were moved to Lake McDonald Lodge and replaced here by three-tiered aluminum chandeliers. There was really no one to object. Louis Hill died in 1948, and with him the passion and understanding of his Glacier/Waterton developments.

While all of the hotels suffered from financial difficulties, the Prince of Wales location at the end of poor roads plagued it. As the economic problems compounded, an unusual alliance between the United States and Canada was growing. The International Rotary Clubs proposed to join Waterton and Glacier as an International Peace Park. In 1932, the peace park was dedicated. As symbolic as the park joining was, it could not stave off the effects of the Depression. In 1933, the railway did not open the hotel for the season. It would remain closed for two seasons, during which it suffered the ravages of neglect and weather. The closure was a blow to the town of Waterton and the Rotarians, but it pushed the completion of the Chief Mountain Highway linking Glacier National Park to Waterton Lakes Park. When the hotel reopened, visitors could more easily drive to the hotel.

The Prince of Wales Hotel, whose namesake never saw the building, is a fitting final monument to Louis Hill. Named a National Historic Site in 1992, it immortalizes Hill's dramatic flair and determination.

Going-to-the-Sun Road, now a National Historic Landmark, offers remarkable park panoramas, above. Mary Roberts Rinehart chats with a cowboy on Piegan Pass in 1932; her prose often accompanied stunning photos in Great Northern promotional brochures such as The Call of the Mountains, *facing page.*

GLACIER NATIONAL PARK & WATERTON LAKES NATIONAL PARK

TOGETHER AN INTERNATIONAL PEACE PARK

The call of the Mountains

Vacations in
Glacier National Park

The Rocky Mountains slice through Glacier National Park and cut across the Canadian border, a spectacular link that pulls together Glacier and Waterton Lakes national parks into the world's first International Peace Park.

Glacier National Park is a masterpiece of nearly 1,600 square miles in northwestern Montana, whose terrain includes glacier-sculpted horns, cirques, arêtes, and hanging valleys interspersed with grasslands, forested hillsides, wildflower-strewn meadows, and alpine tundra highlands. Over thirty glaciers cling to the peaks; their milky waters tumble off rocks, collect in pools, cascade into waterfalls, and fill rock basins to create dozens of lakes.

In old-growth stands of cedar or along ridges cut in stone roams an impressive array of wildlife. Shaggy mountain goats and bighorn sheep dot the cliffs, while mountain lions, lynx, and grizzly and black bears hunt for food, fish in the rivers, or scavenge for huckleberries. White-tailed and mule deer, elk, moose, and an assortment of small mammals such as beavers, muskrats, and minks fill the wild land—the "Crown of the Continent" as explorer, editor, and anthropologist George Bird Grinnell called the park.

For first-time visitors it is an ogler's delight, with one sight to be outdone only by the next. But to those who are hooked, who repeatedly return to Glacier, it is a spiritual experience.

"The call of the mountains draws me back," explained Tessie Bundick, who first came to work at Glacier in 1972 as a college student and returns as a volunteer in the summer. "It's extremely strong. Once you get it into your blood and internalize it, you can't resist the lure of the mountains."

All the more unusual is the ability of visitors to approach Glacier via train. Amtrak's *Empire Builder* still delivers passengers to East Glacier Park Station (Glacier Park Lodge), Essex (Izaak Walton Inn), and Belton Station (West Glacier, Belton Chalet, and Lake McDonald Lodge three miles away), coaxing even the most seasoned traveler back in time. "Time travel" is one element that makes Glacier such an extraordinary experience.

In 1915, popular novelist Mary Roberts Rinehart saddled a horse and, along with a group of riders that included artist Charles

Russell and Theodore Roosevelt hunting companion Howard Eaton, set out for a 300-mile ride through the Rockies of Glacier. As she wrote in *Through Glacier Park,* "…if you love your country; if you like bacon, or will eat it anyhow; if you are willing to learn how little you count in the eternal scheme of things…go ride the Rocky Mountains and save your soul."

Once considered a "saddle packer's park," Glacier still has outfitters who take riders into the backcountry, and most trails are open to horse traffic. Hikers can "save their soul" along 700 miles of trails that introduce them to the diverse delicacies of Glacier, be it via a nature walk or a multi-day trek into the wilderness.

Visitors need not saddle up a horse or tie on hiking boots to have an authentic Glacier experience. The park's original design included a network of roads and boat cruises. Saddle trips, then horse-drawn carriages, took early tourists on their appointed rounds. The first "official" car entered the park in 1914, and soon there were touring cars and buses. By the 1930s, Glacier offered a transportation smorgasbord.

When Going-to-the-Sun Road opened in 1932, visitors who came to the park in private cars could leave from West Glacier and drive through the center of the park over windswept Logan Pass, then down the winding road to St. Mary Lake for an indescribable thrill. Today, 2 million visitors share the adventure as they pilot their vehicles over the two-lane fifty-mile road, now a National Historic Landmark, after it is plowed each summer.

Before national park designation in 1910, sightseers cruised the waters of Lake McDonald, beginning in 1895 aboard the steamboat *F.I. Whitney.* In 1914, J.W. "Cap'n Bill" Swanson established the Swanson Boat Company that eventually became Glacier Park Boat Company. Today, you can take guided boat trips of Lake McDonald, the largest body of water in the park, as well as Lake Josephine, and Swiftcurrent, St. Mary, and Two Medicine lakes. *Chief Two Guns* leaves the dock below Many Glacier Hotel then chugs across Swiftcurrent Lake to a trail to Lake Josephine; from there are trailheads leading to, among other destinations, Grinnell Glacier. Park rangers give interpretive hikes that are nothing short of fantastic.

Fire-engine-red and black "Jammers" are the park's favorite mode of transportation. Early versions of White Motor Company buses began shuttling tourists during the 1914 season, with the red buses going into service in the 1930s. The historic "Jammers," named after the drivers or "gearjammers," were temporarily retired during the 1999 season. Thanks to the efforts of Glacier Park, Inc., the National Park Foundation, Ford Motor Company, and the NPS, the rehabilitated buses are back on the roads, thrilling the "dudes" who flock to the park each summer.

As the park's museum curator, Deirdre Shaw, sees it: "In many ways, because of the hotels, the continuation of the horse packing trips, the boats—many dating from the 1930s—and Jammers, the cultural landscape is very similar to what visitors would have seen forty or fifty years ago. There's a representative slice of that network that's still here."

Chief Mountain International Highway opened in 1936, and Glacier Park visitors could more easily enjoy a Canadian experience. A trip to Waterton Lakes National Park in Alberta only extends the park experience.

Established as a national park by the Canadian government in 1895, Waterton was nearly three decades old when the idea of a "goodwill park" joining Glacier and Waterton first was batted about. Through the efforts of Montana and Alberta Rotarians, in 1932 the International Peace Park was established, the first such park in the

Sightseeing boats cruise Waterton Lakes, facing page, top. Grizzly bears, facing page, and glaciers such as Grinnell Glacier, above, are both synonymous with Glacier National Park.

world. It was named a World Heritage Site in 1995.

The rugged and windswept reaches of Waterton Lakes National Park also exude a natural elegance. Perhaps the long fingers of the lakes against the mountains or the perfectly appointed peaks draped in lush foliage give it an air not found across the border.

Tour boats ply the waters, offering a perfect way to wallow in this remarkable fifty-four-square-mile swatch of natural diversity. Here prairie plants overlap with coastal flora; more than half of Alberta's plant species can be found in Waterton.

The park is a birder's paradise, with over 250 species of winged wildlife. In late fall, you can

watch waterfowl, along with golden eagles, migrate through Waterton. Over sixty species of mammals including bighorn sheep, elk, deer, grizzly and black bears, and a small herd of bison that make their home near the north entrance, thrive here.

Unlike in U.S. national parks, townsites exist within Canada's national parks, and Waterton Townsite is a quaint collection of homes, shops, and restaurants. While the park is open year-round, most facilities close for the winter and the summer population of 2,000 dwindles to 100 hardy souls.

The International Peace Park brings together two remarkable national treasures along the world's longest undefended border.

PRESERVATION RESOURCES
FOR PRESERVATION OF NATIONAL PARK HISTORIC STRUCTURES

Lake McDonald Lodge in Glacier National Park underwent extensive restoration and rehabilitation in the late 1980s, bringing back spaces like the dining room to their original glory.

Here are some of the non-profit organizations that support programs within the parks. Many have specific projects related to historic buildings.

Friends of Crater Lake National Park
P.O. Box 88
Crater Lake, OR 97604
www.halcyon.com/rdpayne/
foclnp.html
Cooperates with the National Park Service in the stewardship of the park's natural and cultural resources.

Friends of Timberline
333 SW Taylor
Portland, OR 97204
(503) 295-0827
www.timberlinelodge.com
Responsible for the fundraising that enables Timberline's priceless handmade furniture and accessories to be restored or replicated.

Glacier Park Foundation
P.O. Box 15641
Minneapolis, MN 55415
www.spacestar.net/users/skyward/
gpf97
Founded by former Glacier Park employees and visitors, the foundation's interests are in park history and traditions, and visitor facilities.

The Glacier Fund
Glacier National Park
West Glacier, MT 59936
(406) 888-7910
www.nps.gov/glac/home.htm
Holds restricted accounts for wildlife research, historic building restoration, environmental education, backcountry trails, and facilities that include Sperry and Granite Park chalets.

Glacier National Park Associates
Box 91
Kalispell, MT 59903
www.nps.gov/glac/partners/gnpa.htm
An advocacy group to help the park accomplish its goals for which park funding is insufficient, and educate the public about biological, geological, cultural, and historical resources of the park.

Glacier Natural History Association
P.O. Box 310
West Glacier, MT 59936
(406) 888-5756
Housed in the historic Belton Depot in West Glacier, GNHA helps support the park's educational, interpretive, cultural, and scientific program needs.

Grand Canyon Association
P.O. Box 399
Grand Canyon, AZ 86023
(520) 638-2481
www.grandcanyon.org
Supports education, research, and other programs for the benefit of Grand Canyon National Park and its visitors.

Grand Canyon National Park Foundation
23 East Fine Ave.
Flagstaff, AZ 86001
(520) 774-1760
www.grandcanyonfoundation.org
Funds projects and programs that enhance, restore, or further protect the park's natural and cultural resources or improve the quality of the visitor experience.

National Park Foundation
1101 17th Street NW, Suite 1102
Washington, DC 20036-4704
www.nationalparks.org/npf
Protects natural habitats and preserves our historic and cultural sites in the national parks.

National Trust for Historic Preservation
1785 Massachusetts Ave. NW
Washington, DC 20036
(202) 588-6000
www.nationaltrust.org
Preservation information, events, and activism for America's historic places.

National Trust for Historic Preservation
Mountains/Plains Regional Office
910 16th St., Suite 1100
Denver, CO 80202
(303) 623-1504
www.nthp.org/main/frontline/
regions/mountains.org
(Covers CO, KS, MT, NE, ND, SD, WY)
Established a dedicated fund for restoration of national park historic structures.

National Trust for Historic Preservation
Western Regional Office
One Sutter St., Suite 707
San Francisco, CA 94104
(415) 956-0610
(Covers AK, AZ, CA, NV, OR, UT, WA)

Yellowstone Association
P.O. Box 117
Yellowstone National Park, WY 82190
(307) 344-2294
www.yellowstoneassociation.org
Funds and provides educational products and services for Yellowstone National Park.

The Yellowstone Park Foundation
Story Building
37 Main St., Suite 4
Bozeman, MT 59715
(406) 586-6303
www.ypf.org

Yosemite Association
P.O. Box 230
El Portal, CA 95318
(209) 379-2646
www.yosemite.org
Supports interpretive, educational, research, scientific, and environmental programs in Yosemite National Park.

Yosemite Fund
155 Montgomery St., Suite 1104
San Francisco, CA 94104
(415) 434-1782
www.yosemitefund.org
The primary non-profit fundraising organization for Yosemite National Park that funds projects in the park that government funds can't cover.

TRAVELERS' RESOURCES

FOR RESERVATIONS AT THE GREAT LODGES

The Ahwahnee Hotel
Yosemite National Park
1 Ahwahnee Road
Yosemite, CA 95389
Hotel reservations (209) 372-0200
Fax (209) 372-1463
www.webportal.com/ahwahnee
Season: Open year round. Contact the park service or The Ahwahnee for road conditions. YARTS buses run from gateway communities outside the park into Yosemite Valley.

Belton Chalet
P.O. Box 206
West Glacier, MT 59937
Hotel reservations (406) 888-5000
Fax (406) 888-5005
www.beltonchalet.com
Season: Early July to early September. Amtrak arrives daily at Belton Depot across Highway 2 from Belton Chalet at West Glacier. Call 800-872-7254 for train reservations.

Bryce Canyon Lodge
Bryce Canyon National Park
1 Bryce Canyon
Bryce Canyon, UT 84717
Hotel reservations (888) 297-2757
Direct to hotel (435) 834-5361
Fax (435) 834-5464
www.brycecanyonlodge.com
Season: Mid-April to late October. Contact the park service for current shuttle information.

Bryce Canyon National Park
P.O. Box 17001
Bryce Canyon, UT 84717
Visitor phone (425) 834-5322
E-mail:
BRCA_Superintendant@nps.gov
www.nps.gov/brca

Crater Lake Lodge
Crater Lake National Park
P.O. Box 158
Crater Lake, OR 97604
Hotel reservations (541) 830-8700
Fax (541) 830-8514
www.craterlakelodges.com
Season: Mid-May to late October. Contact park service or lodge for road information.

Crater Lake National Park
P.O. Box 7
Crater Lake, OR 97604
Visitor information (541) 594-3000
E-mail: Craterlake_Info@nps.gov
www.nps.gov/crla

El Tovar
Grand Canyon National Park
P.O. Box 694
Grand Canyon, AZ 86023
Hotel reservations (888) 297-2757
Fax (520) 638-9810
www.grandcanyonlodges.com
Season: Open year round. Grand Canyon Railway runs daily from Williams, AZ, to the Grand Canyon Depot on the South Rim. (800) 843-8724 or www.thetrain.com. Contact the park for current public transit information.

Glacier National Park
Park Headquarters
West Glacier, MT 59936
Visitor phone (406) 888-7800
E-mail: glac_park_info@nps.gov
www.nps.gov/glac

Glacier Park Lodge
Glacier National Park
106 Way, Suite 184
East Glacier, MT 59936
Hotel reservations (406) 756-2444
Fax (406) 257-0384
E-mail: info@glacierparkinc.com
www.glacierparkinc.com
Season: Mid-May to mid-October. Amtrak travels to the park daily and stops at Glacier Park Station; call 800-872-7254.

Grand Canyon Lodge
Grand Canyon National Park
Grand Canyon North Rim, AZ 86052
Hotel reservations (888) 297-2757
Fax (520) 638-2534
www.grandcanyonnorthrim.com
Season: Mid-May to mid-October.

Grand Canyon National Park
P.O. Box 129
Grand Canyon, AZ 86023
Visitor phone (520) 638-7888
E-mail:
GRCA_Superintendent@nps.gov
www.nps.gov/grca

Granite Park Chalet
Glacier Wilderness Guides/Montana
Raft Company
P.O. Box 330
West Glacier, MT 59936
Hotel reservations (406) 387-5555
Fax (406) 387-5656
E-mail: glguides@cyberport.net
www.glacierguides.com
Season: Early July to mid-September. Trail access is from Many Glacier Hotel. Directions provided with reservations.

Lake McDonald Lodge
Glacier National Park
P.O. Box 210052
Lake McDonald, MT 59921
Hotel reservations (406) 755-6303
Fax (406) 257-0384
E-mail: info@glacierparkinc.com
www.glacierparkinc.com
Season: Late May to early October. Lake McDonald is about 3 miles from the West Glacier entrance and Belton Depot, which has daily Amtrak service.

Many Glacier Hotel
Glacier National Park
Midvale Road #1
East Glacier Park, MT 59434
Hotel reservations (406) 755-6303
Fax (406) 257-0384
E-mail:info@glacierparkinc.com
www.glacierparkinc.com
Season: Early June to mid-September.

Mount Hood National Forest
Headquarters Office
16400 Champion Way
Sandy, OR 97055
Visitor information (503) 622-7674

Mount Rainier National Park
Tahoma Woods, Star Route
Ashford, WA 98304-9751
Visitor phone (360) 569-2211, ext. 3314
E-mail: MORAInfo@nps.gov
www.nps.gov/mora

Old Faithful Inn
Yellowstone National Park
P.O. Box 2130
Old Faithful Station
Yellowstone National Park, WY 82190

Hotel reservations (307) 344-7311
Fax (307) 344-7456
www.travelyellowstone.com
Season: Mid-May to mid-October. Adjacent Snow Lodge open mid-December to early March. Check with lodge or park for road information.

Oregon Caves Chateau
Oregon Caves National Monument
20000 Caves Highway
Caves Junction, OR 97523
Hotel reservations (541) 592-3400
www.southwestoregon.com
Season: Mid-March to early December.

Oregon Caves National Monument
19000 Caves Highway
Cave Junction, OR 97523
Visitor phone (541) 592-2100
www.nps.gov/orca

Paradise Inn
Mount Rainier National Park
Paradise, WA 98398
Hotel reservations (360) 569-2275
Fax (360) 569-2770
www.guestservices.com/rainier/
Season: Mid-May to early October.

Prince of Wales Hotel
Waterton Lakes National Park
Alberta, Canada TOK 2MO
Hotel reservations (403) 859-2231
Fax (403) 859-2630
E-mail: info@glacierparkinc.com
www.glacierparkinc.com
Season: Mid-May to early October.

Sperry Chalet
Glacier National Park
P.O. Box 188
West Glacier, MT 59936
Hotel reservations (406) 387-5654
www.sperrychalet.com
Season: Early July to early September. Trail access is from Lake McDonald. Directions provided with reservations.

Timberline Lodge
Timberline Lodge, OR 97028
Hotel reservations (800) 547-1406
Fax (503) 622-0710
www.timberlinelodge.com
Season: Open year-round.

Waterton Lakes National Park
Alberta, Canada TOK 2MO
Visitor phone (406) 756-2444
E-mail: info@glacierparkinc.com
www.glacierparkinc.com

Yellowstone National Park
P.O. Box 168
Yellowstone National Park, WY 82190-0168
Visitor phone (307) 344-7381
E-mail: yell_visitor_services@nps.gov
www.nps.gov/yell

Yosemite National Park
Superintendent
P.O. Box 577
Yosemite National Park, CA 95389
Visitor phone (209) 372-0200
E-mail: yose_web_manager@nps.gov
www.nps.gov/yose

Zion National Park
SR 9
Springdale, UT 84767
Visitor phone (435) 772-3256
E-mail:
ZION_park_information@nps.gov
www.nps.gov/zion

Zion Park Lodge
Zion National Park
Springdale, Utah 84767
Hotel reservations (888) 297-2757
Fax (435) 772-2001
www.zionlodge.com
Season: Open year-round. Call the park service for current shuttle information.

For further lodge information, and other books by Christine Barnes, check: www.greatlodges.com

Public Broadcasting System website for the television series is: PBS.org/GreatLodges

JELECTED BIBLIOGRAPHY & JOURCEJ

In preparing this book, I consulted a great many sources, among which were: Historic Structure Reports, Preservation Architectural Guides, Resources Studies and Surveys, Furnishings Reports, National Register of Historic Places Inventory Nomination Forms, and Historic American Buildings Reports prepared for or by the Department of the Interior, National Park Service, on individual parks and buildings. Some are listed here, and I am grateful to the authors and editors of all of them.

Publications

Adams, Ansel. *Ansel Adams: An Autobiography*. Boston: Little, Brown, 1985.

Albright, Horace, and Robert Cahn. *The Birth of the National Park Service: The Founding Years, 1913-33*. Salt Lake City: Howe Brothers, 1985.

Anderson, Michael, F. *Living at the Edge*. Grand Canyon: Grand Canyon Association, 1998.

Arizona Daily Sun. April 1, Sept. 8, 1975, Nov. 1, 1981.

Bartlett, Richard. *Yellowstone: A Wilderness Besieged*. Tucson: University of Arizona Press, 1985.

Buchholtz, C.W. *Man in Glacier*. West Glacier, MT: Glacier Natural History Association, 1976.

Caywood, Janene, and Frank Grant. *Inventory and Evaluation of Historical Resources Within Bryce Canyon National Park*. Missoula: HRS, Inc., 1994.

Clemensen, A. Berle. *Historic Structure Report: Old Faithful Inn, Yellowstone National Park*. Denver: National Park Service, 1982.

Djuff, Ray. "Glacier on Wheels: A History of the Park Buses," *The Inside Trail*, Vol. XII No. 2 (Fall 1999), Vol. XIII No. 1 (Winter 2000), Vol. XIII No. 2 (Summer 2000).

—. *The Prince of Wales Hotel*. Calgary, Alberta: Rocky Mountain Press, 1991.

Friends of Timberline. *Timberline Lodge: A Guided Tour*. Portland, OR: Friends of Timberline, 1991.

Fraley, John. *A Woman's Way West: In and Around Glacier National Park from 1925 to 1990*. Whitefish, MT: Big Mountain Publishing, 1998.

Fulton, Eleanor. *Timberline Lodge*. Historic American Buildings Survey, OR-161. Washington, D.C.: National Park Service, 1995.

Grattan, Virginia L. *Mary Colter: Builder upon the Red Earth*. Flagstaff, AZ: Northland Press, 1980.

Griffin, Rachael, and Sarah Munro, eds. *Timberline Lodge*. Portland, OR: Friends of Timberline, 1978.

Haines, Aubrey L. *The Yellowstone Story: A History of Our First National Park*. 2 vols. Boulder: University of Colorado Press, 1977.

Harrison, Laura Soulliere. *Architecture in the Parks: National Historic Landmark Theme Study*. National Park Service, Washington, D.C.: 1986.

Hubbard, Freeman. *Encyclopedia of North American Railroading: 150 Years of Railroading in the United States and Canada*. New York: McGraw-Hill, 1981.

Hughes, Donald, J. *In the House of Stone and Light*. Grand Canyon, AZ: Grand Canyon Natural History Association, 1991.

Hyde, Anne Farrar. *An American Vision: Far Western Landscape and National Culture, 1820-1920*. New York and London: New York University Press, 1990.

Juillerat, Lee. *Lodge of the Imagination: The Crater Lake Lodge Story*. Crater Lake, OR: Crater Lake Natural History Association, 1995.

Kaiser, Harvey H. *Landmarks in the Landscape*. San Francisco: Chronicle Books, 1997.

Kreisman, "Curtain Up." *The Seattle Times/Post Intelligencer*, Pacific Edition, May 6, 1990.

Leavengood, David. "The Mountain Architecture of R.C. Reamer," *Mountain Gazette*, June 1976.

Lomazzi, Brad S. *Railroad Timetables, Travel Brochures & Posters*. Spencertown: Gold Hill Press, 1995.

McDonald, James. *Granite Park Chalet, Glacier National Park: Historic Preservation Architectural Guide*. Denver: National Park Service, 1985.

—. *Lake McDonald Lodge, Glacier National Park: Historic Preservation Architectural Guide*. Denver: National Park Service, 1984, revised 1985.

—. *Many Glacier Hotel, Glacier National Park: Architectural Preservation Guide*. Denver: National Park Service, 1984.

—. *Sperry Chalet, Glacier National Park: Historic Preservation Architectural Guide*. Denver: National Park Service, 1985.

Guests enjoy fine cuisine and a superb view in El Tovar's Canyon Dining Room.

—. *Zion Lodge and Birch Creek Historic District, Zion National Park, Utah: Historic Structures Report*. Missoula, MT: TWRS Recreational Services and National Park Service, 1997.

Mark, Stephen R. *Administrative History*. Chapter 17, "Planning and Development at Rim Village, Crater Lake National Park." Seattle: National Park Service, 1991.

—. *Oregon Caves Chateau*. Historic American Buildings Survey, OR-145. Denver: National Park Service, 1989.

Matthews, Henry. *Kirtland Cutter*. Seattle: University of Washington Press, 1998.

Moylan, Bridget. *Glacier's Grandest*. Missoula, MT: Pictorial Histories Publishing, 1995.

Muir, John. *The Yosemite*. New York: Sierra Club Books, 1912.

Richmond, Al. *The Story of the Grand Canyon Railway*. Third printing. Flagstaff, AZ: Grand Canyon Railway. 1995.

Rinehart, Mary Roberts. *Through Glacier Park in 1915*. P.F. Collier & Son, Inc., 1916. Reprint ed., Boulder, CO: Roberts Rinehart, 1983.

Robinson, Donald H. *Through the Years in Glacier National Park*. Location not given: Glacier Natural History Association and National Park Service, 1960.

Rose, Judith, ed. *Timberline Lodge: A Love Story*. Portland, OR: Graphic Arts Center Publishing and Friends of Timberline, 1986.

Runte, Alfred. *Trains of Discovery*. 4th ed. Boulder, CO: Roberts Rinehart, 1998.

Sargent, Shirley. *The Ahwahnee Hotel*. Santa Barbara: Sequoia Communications, 1990.

Sceva, Paul H. *Recollections by the Old Man of the Mountain*. Tacoma, WA: By the author, 1974.

Schmidt, Jeremy, Thomas Schmidt, and Art Wolfe. *The Smithsonian Guides to Natural America: The Northern Rockies*. New York: Smithsonian Books, 1995.

Scrattish, Nicholas. *Historic Resource Study: Bryce Canyon National Park*. Denver: National Park Service, 1985.

Snow, David. *Historic Structure Report: Mount Rainier, Paradise Inn*. Denver: National Park Service, 1978.

Spencer, Jeannette Dyer. *Ahwahnee, Yosemite National Park, California*. Location not given: The Yosemite Park & Curry, 1942.

Staehli, Alfred, AIA. *A Position Paper on Crater Lake Lodge, Crater Lake National Park*. Salem: The Historic Preservation League of Oregon, 1986.

Tweed, William, Laura E. Soulliere, and Henry G. Law. *National Park Service Rustic Architecture: 1916-1942*. Washington, D.C.: National Park Service, Western Regional Office, 1977.

Vaughan, Thomas, and Virginia Ferriday, eds. *Space, Style and Structure: Building in Northwest America*. 2 vols. Portland: Oregon Historical Society, 1974.

Weir, Jean B. *Timberline Lodge: A WPA Experiment in Architecture and Crafts*. 2 vols. Ann Arbor: University of Michigan, 1977.

Woodbury, Angus M. "A History of Southern Utah and its National Parks." *Utah Historical Quarterly*, Vol. 12 No. 3 (July 1944), No. 4 (Oct. 1944).

Zaitlin, Joyce. *Gilbert Stanley Underwood: His Rustic, Art Deco, and Federal Architecture*. Malibu, CA: Pangloss Press, 1989.

Materials from Park, Corporate, and Private Archives

Bryce Canyon National Park Archives, Bryce Canyon, Utah. Correspondence and brochures from Union Pacific Railroad Archives, Omaha (microfiche). Partnership in Preservation active maintenance files. State of Utah and Utah Parks Company correspondence. Superintendent's Annual Reports. UPC and BCNP correspondence. Utah Parks Company contract, 1923.

Crater Lake National Park Archives and Library, Crater Lake, Oregon. Lium, Robert: personal memoirs. National Park Service, Fletcher Farr Ayotte, Architects, CH2MHill, Consulting Engineers: "Rehabilitation of Historic Crater Lake Lodge, Comprehensive Design Program, Historic Character/Documentation," March 30, 1990. Staehli, Alfred, AIA, "Crater Lake Lodge: Additional Notes on Its Architectural Significance and About the Architect," prepared for The Historic Preservation League of Oregon, January 1988.

Croft, George A. "Establishment of North Rim Facilities." Unpublished memoirs, courtesy of Carl Croft.

Federal Records Center, Sand Point, Washington. Mount Rainier National Park Superintendent's reports and correspondence, 1915-1919.

Friends of Timberline, Portland, Oregon. Correspondence: Presidential Dedication Visit to Mt. Hood. Smith, Margery Hoffman, "The Interior Design of Timberline Lodge," n.d.

Glacier National Park Archives and Library, West Glacier, Montana. AmFac, Inc. press release, July 10, 1968. Architectural drawings Nos. 8175, 8200, 8089, 8175. Correspondence boxes 76, 85, 97. Correspondence files, 1911-16. Glacier Park Hotel Co. Bulletin #4, July 15, 1914. Great Northern Railway promotional brochures. Superintendent's annual and monthly reports, 1911-14.

Grand Canyon National Park Library and Archives, Grand Canyon, Arizona. Correspondence: Atchison, Topeka & Santa Fe, 1902-11. Fred Harvey Collection: 1889-1963, Fred Harvey Company. Grand Canyon Lodge, North Rim file: *The Hotel in the Wilderness*. History file: *El Tovar: A New Hotel at the Grand Canyon of Arizona,* 1909, *Hotel El Tovar,* 1905, *Titan of the Chasms: The Grand Canyon of Arizona,* 1904, *Doing the Grand Canyon,* 1909. Superintendent's Annual Reports, 1926-28, 1932, 1936. Union Pacific Railroad promotional brochures.

Minnesota Historical Society, St. Paul, Minnesota. Great Northern Railway, President's File. Great Northern Railway Co. Records: Glacier Park Division, Old Subject Files, Glacier Park Co. and Glacier Park Co., Canadian Div.

Mount Hood National Forest, Zig Zag Ranger Station, OR. Forrest, Linn: oral history, 1978. Gano, Ward: "Some Timberline Lodge Recollections," July, 21, 1978. Olmsted, Frederick, Jr.: Design File, letters of Feb. 18, March 14, 1931. "Report on Forest Service Activities in Connection with the Visit of the President's Party to Mt. Hood National Forest, Sept. 28, 1937." U.S. Forest Service: "Notes on the Progress of Timberline Lodge."

Mount Rainier National Park, Tahoma Woods and Longmire, WA. Allaback, Sarah: "The Rustic Furnishings of Mount Rainier National Park, 1916-1966," Historic American Buildings Survey, September 1996.

Oland, Douglas. Personal memoirs, courtesy of the Oland family, Waterton, Alberta, Canada.

Oregon Caves National Monument, Oregon Caves, Oregon. Interpretation Division Files, General Data: History of Oregon Caves National Monument, 1849-1989. *Grants Pass Courier* articles. History Files: Correspondence. *San Francisco Examiner* articles.

Tacoma Public Library, WA. Northwest Collection: *Tacoma Ledger* articles on development at Mount Rainier National Park, Dec. 12, 17, 1911, June 27, 1915, Sept. 24, 1916. *Tacoma Tribune* articles on development at Mount Rainier National Park, Feb. 13, Sept. 14, 1916.

Technical Information Center, National Park Service, Denver Service Center, Denver, Colorado. Architectural drawings and blueprints.

White, Jane Reamer. 1970 correspondence to Richard Bartlett. Courtesy of Richard Bartlett.

Yellowstone National Park Archives, Mammoth, Wyoming. Letter box #39, file #10: accommodations at hotels and camps. Superintendent's Annual Reports. *Through Wonderland,* Northern Pacific Railway brochure, 1905. YPC: Volume 3 (furniture), Inventory, Sept. 30, 1929, The American Appraisal Co. YPC-14: lodges and camps: 1932-37. YPC-34: business correspondence: 1934-36. YPC-126: Old Faithful Inn, 1959. YPHCo.: 1925-27, Box C-14, file 332.2.

Yosemite National Park Research Library and Records Center, Yosemite, California. #11130: Underwood, Gilbert Stanley, Specification for the Ahwahnee Hotel. "Ahwahnee: Yosemite's New Hotel," *National Motor,* August 1927, Box #79. The Ahwahnee Hotel file: YPCC minutes of Board of Directors, Box #8, Correspondence and memos, Box #79. "History of the United States Naval Special Hospital," Yosemite National Park, Yosemite Park & Curry Co., Jan. 15, 1946.

Zion National Park Archives, Utah. Superintendent's Annual Reports.

Members of the Los Angeles Chamber of Commerce pose in all their travel finery on the edge of the Grand Canyon in 1906.

PHOTOGRAPH & ILLUSTRATION CREDITS

Color Photographs

Fred Pflughoft & David Morris: 1, 9, 10, 19 left, 20, 21 left, 22, 34, 36, 37, 38-39, 40 right, 41, 53, 54 all, 55, 56, 62 bottom, 63, 66 left, 67 right, 68, 69, 76, 78, 79 all, 89, 90, 93, 104, 106 bottom, 107, 129 bottom, 130, 131, 150, 161, 162, 163 bottom, 175 both, 181, 186, 188, 191

David Morris: 6 right, 6-7 background, 19 right, 23, 35, 48, 48-49 background, 57, 58, 60, 60-61 background, 62 top, 71, 73, 74, 82, 83 both, 92 bottom, 95 top, 96, 97 both, 98-99, 100-101 background, 103 top left, 110, 111, 112, 113, 135, 136, 140, 141 both, 142-143, 148 bottom, 152-153 background, 158-159 background, 170, 177 top left and right, 192

Fred Pflughoft: 2-3, 4-5, 6 left, 7 both, 14, 14-15 background, 16 top, 17, 24 bottom, 26, 27 both, 28, 29 right, 30, 46-47, 72, 74-75 background, 77, 81, 84, 84-85 background, 91, 94, 95 bottom, 100, 108 bottom, 114-115 background, 120 all, 121, 122, 123, 124-125, 125 right, 126, 126-127 background, 132 both, 134, 136-137 background, 144, 146, 151, 158, 165 both, 173, 177 bottom, 178, 178-179 background, 184 top

Amfac Parks & Resorts: 109
Courtesy of Andy Beck: 24 top
Fletcher Farr Ayotte: 92 top
Andrew Geiger: 152, 156 all
Bert Gildart: 168 top, 169 bottom
Chuck Haney: 147 bottom, 157 both, 185
John L. Hinderman: 29 left, 59, 184 bottom
Robert Holmes: 40 left
John Reddy: 170-171 background
RLK Company: 70
Keith S. Walklet: 8, 12-13, 30-31, 42, 43 both, 44 both, 45
Garry Wunderwald: 166, 166-167 background, 182

HISTORIC PHOTOS & DRAWINGS

Bryce Canyon National Park: 127; 128, 129 top, 133
Harry Christensen: 80 top
Colorado Historical Society: 16 bottom, 21 right
Crater Lake National Park: 86, 87 top, 88
Eastern Washington State Historical Society: 159
Friends of Timberline: 61; 64 top, 65 top and bottom, 66 right, 67 left
Glacier National Park Museum: 145, 155 bottom, 147 top and inset, 160 bottom, 163 bottom, 167, 168 bottom, 171, 174 top, 180 both, 183 both
Glacier Natural History Association: 160
Grand Canyon National Park Museum: 101, 102, 103 top right, 105, 106 top, 108 top, 137, 138 top left and right, 138 both, 139 top, 169 top, 172 top, 189
Grand Canyon Railway: 103 bottom left & right
James J. Hill Reference Library, St. Paul, MN.: 144-145 background, 148 left, 148 right top, 153, 154
Bob Jacobs Collection: 155 top
Klamath County Museum: 87 bottom
Brad S. Lomazzi Collection: 18
Minnesota Historical Society: 172 bottom, 174 bottom
Montana Historical Society: 15
Mount Rainier National Park: 50 left, 50 right, 51, 52
National Park Service, Yellowstone National Park: 25
National Park Service, Denver Service Center: 31*, 49
Oregon Caves National Monument: 75, 80 bottom
Oregon Historical Society: 64 bottom, 85
Parks Canada: 179
Union Pacific Railroad: 115, 116, 118
Yosemite Museum, National Park Service: 32 left and right, 33
Zion National Park: 114; 117 both; 119 top and bottom

Illustrations

Linda McCray: map and end pages

* Redrawn by Linda McCray from damaged historical documents

INDEX

Views are always spectacular even from some bathtubs such as this one at Crater Lake Lodge.

Following page:
Many Glacier Hotel, set in a pocket of glacial splendor, Glacier National Park, Montana.